A

SAINSBURY COOKBOOK

—

STUDENTS'

COOKBOOK

EASY RECIPES FOR HOME LEAVERS

ɔSON

D1634459

CONTENTS

Published exclusively for J Sainsbury plc
Stamford House Stamford Street
London SE1 9LL
by Martin Books
Simon & Schuster Consumer Group
Grafton House 64 Maids Causeway
Cambridge CB5 8DD

First published 1992
Second impression January 1993

ISBN 0 85941 802 2

Text © 1992, Sophie Grigson
Illustrations © 1992, J Sainsbury plc
Photographs © 1992, Jess Koppel

Printed in Italy by Printer Trento

THE AUTHOR

Born in 1959, Sophie Grigson spent her childhood in England and in France, where the cuisine inspired in her an early interest in food.

Sophie has travelled widely, in South East Asia, the United States, South America and India, but she is particularly fond of Italy, a country she now revisits every year.

Currently cookery writer for London's *Evening Standard*, Sophie also contributes to other newspapers and magazines. Her previous publications include *Sophie's Table*, *Sophie Grigson's Ingredients Book*, and *Food for Friends*.

Pictured on the front cover: Keema Pilau (Minced Meat Pilau, page 32)
Pictured on the back cover: Stir-fried Vegetables (page 72)

INTRODUCTION

*All recipes in this book
give ingredients in both
metric (g, ml, etc.) and
imperial (oz, pints, etc.)
measures. Use either set of
quantities, but not both,
in any one recipe.*

*All teaspoons and
tablespoons are level,
unless otherwise stated. 1
teaspoon = a 5 ml spoon;
1 tablespoon = a 15 ml
spoon.*

*Egg size is medium
(size 3) unless otherwise
stated.*

*Vegetables are medium
size, unless otherwise
stated.*

*Freshly ground black
pepper and fresh herbs
should be used, unless
otherwise stated.*

Moving away from home, into your own flat or
bedsit, sharing or solo, can be tremendously
exciting. For the first time you are an
independent adult. There's no one to tell you to
tidy your room, you can stay out until all hours
on Saturday night and spend all of Sunday in
bed. Freedom! But with freedom comes
responsibility. Suddenly you've got to deal with
bills and cleaning and laundry, and on top of
that you've got to feed yourself. Of course, you
could live on a diet of reheated frozen and
packaged ready-made meals, take-aways, and
beans on toast. Why bother to cook when there
is so much else to be done?

The best reason for cooking your own meals,
and the one that motivated me most when I
moved into my first bedsit, is that cooking is
fun, and comes with the added bonus that you
end up with something great to eat. Beans on
toast and take-away pizzas are fine once in a
while, but there's much more satisfaction to be
gained from cooking a meal from scratch. There
are also two good practical reasons. Firstly,
ready-made meals and take-aways are more
expensive than home-cooked food, and
secondly, meals based on fresh foods are usually
the best option health-wise.

When it comes down to it, anyone who likes
to eat can learn to cook well. It's just a question
of learning the basics and building up your
repertoire from there. Like any other skill, it gets
easier with practice. Sure, you'll make mistakes
along the way: every cook, however experienced,
does. The important thing is to learn from the
occasional disaster and not to let it throw you off
stride. Relax and enjoy yourself in the kitchen;
cooking is a pleasure and a skill that you will
benefit from for the rest of your life.

This is not an absolute beginners' book. I've
assumed that you have been in a kitchen before,
and that you can work out for yourself how to
boil a potato. However, even if your culinary

Preparation and cooking times

Preparation and cooking times are included at the head of the recipes as a general guide; preparation times, especially, are approximate and timings are usually rounded to the nearest 5 minutes.

Preparation times include the time taken to prepare ingredients in the list, but not to make any 'basic' recipe, such as a sauce.

The cooking times given at the heads of the recipes denote cooking periods when the dish can be left largely unattended, e.g. baking, stewing, and not the total amount of cooking for the recipe. Always read and follow the timings given for the steps of the recipe in the method.

experience is minimal, you should be able to tackle most of the recipes without difficulty. There's a glossary of kitchen techniques on page 13 which should answer most queries about particular culinary terms. Nine times out of ten, common sense will help with small uncertainties. How small should you chop an onion? Well, how big do you want the bits to be in the final dish? If in doubt, stop and think. Don't be daunted by what may seem a complicated recipe; take it step by step, and you'll find that it isn't impossible at all. Above all, never panic in the kitchen; a cool head is your best ally when something goes wrong. It's not the end of the world if your dish doesn't turn out quite right.

When using a recipe, remember that the cooking times given should always be treated as approximate, so check for 'doneness' by eye or by taste. Ovens vary, and your oven's 200°C, or whatever, may be a degree or two hotter or colder than mine. Similarly, your interpretation of a medium heat may not be quite the same as mine. Check that you've got the seasoning right by tasting wherever practical.

KITCHENS AND KITCHEN EQUIPMENT

SHARING A KITCHEN

The two biggest bones of contention in a shared home are the telephone bill and the kitchen. At least the telephone bill is a nightmare you'll only have to negotiate quarterly. The kitchen, on the other hand, can be a continual problem. Ease the friction by showing consideration for your flat-mates, and attempt to instil the same attitude in them.

Most importantly, always keep the kitchen clean. A dirty kitchen is a potential health hazard; germs will breed willy-nilly in a neglected kitchen, and more obvious wildlife, such as ants, mice, cockroaches and others might be tempted in. Splatters of food or fat on the floor should be wiped up instantly, otherwise you're likely to slip on them, which could be serious, particularly if you are carrying a dish of boiling hot food at the time. Clean the fridge and the oven regularly and don't leave dirty dishes in the sink; wash up utensils as you cook, if possible, then there's less to do later. Always wash knives and chopping boards after preparing raw meats and before using them for other ingredients.

Store raw meats in the fridge, but below or well away from cooked meats and raw vegetables. Throw out any foods that are mouldering at the back of the fridge, or are past their use-by date. The same goes for anything that smells even mildly suspect: use your common sense and don't take risks.

Clean up straightaway after you've been cooking, and leave the kitchen neat and tidy. Unless you cook communally, it's worth labelling your shopping so there's less chance of an ownership dispute. If you do cook communally, don't shirk on your share of the cooking, washing-up or food bills. Remember that if there is a problem of kitchen habits, it is best to tackle it as soon and as diplomatically as possible, before it has a chance to escalate into a major dispute.

LIMITED FACILITIES

The equipment and facilities in a rented kitchen are unlikely to be top-notch, but it is amazing what you can do with limited resources. In terms of facilities, the very least you need are a couple of electric or gas rings that work and a functional fridge. If you also have a grill and an oven, then you can tackle most things, no problem. Ovens can be temperamental, so accept the fact that it may take a little while to get used to the quirks of yours, and that your results may be less than perfect in the mean time. If your kitchen is of the shoe-box variety, then tidiness and good organisation while you work are of even more importance than in a generously proportioned room.

Build up your own collection of equipment as you can afford it. By and large, the higher the price the better the quality and the longer it will last, so think of kitchen purchases as long-term investments. Treat your kitchen equipment well, following manufacturers' instructions for cleaning and care, and make sure that flat-mates do the same.

KITCHEN EQUIPMENT

ABSOLUTELY ESSENTIAL ITEMS

BOWLS: *ideally you should have at least three of different sizes, and a big one that is presentable enough to use as a salad bowl is doubly useful. However, you can mix ingredients in any large enough bowl; there is no need to buy mixing bowls specially.*

CAN OPENER

CASSEROLE: *a medium-size ovenproof casserole with a lid, for cooking stews, baking puddings, etc., can double as a serving-dish for vegetables, rice, etc. Flameproof casseroles tend to be more expensive, but have the advantage that they can be used on the hob as well as in the oven, especially useful if you haven't even got an oven.*

CHOPPING BOARDS: *one large chopping board is more useful than two or three small ones. If it is wooden, wipe it down after use, but don't leave it to soak, as wooden boards can split as they dry, and in any case take ages to dry out. Plastic and melamine boards are hygienic and easy to clean.*

FRYING PAN: *a large frying-pan, about 25 cm (10 inches) across, is essential, the heavier and thicker the better. This is useful for making small stews as well as for frying. Smaller frying-pans are handy for frying individual eggs or small amounts of onion, etc.*

FISH SLICE: *for lifting all kinds of foods, not just fish.*

GRATER: *a square box grater is sturdy and easy to use.*

SAUCEPANS: *you will need at least two, and preferably three, of varying sizes. The heavier and thicker the metal, the better.*

SHARP KNIVES: *the most vital pieces of equipment in any kitchen. You'll need at least one small knife for preparing vegetables and one large one (with about a 15 cm (6-inch) blade) for slicing larger things. Knives*

should be sharp enough to slice through an onion as if it were a pat of butter.

SIEVE: *you can manage with one large, sturdy sieve which can be used for draining vegetables, rinsing and draining rice and pasta, or sieving soups and purées. If you have a metal sieve, it can also be used as a steamer, and is more heat-resistant than plastic.*

SPOONS: *wooden or otherwise, you'll need something for stirring.*

NOT ESSENTIAL BUT VERY USEFUL ITEMS

AIRTIGHT STORAGE CONTAINERS: *for flour, sugar, dried beans, rice, etc. Storage containers can be large screw-top jars, plastic ice cream cartons or purpose-made storage containers: anything will do as long as it is airtight. Polythene bags or open packets of rice or pasta can be sealed with clothes pegs or rubber bands.*

BAKING SHEETS: *useful for cookies and biscuits.*

CITRUS JUICER

COLANDER: *better for draining large quantities of vegetables, etc., than a sieve, and useful for salting aubergines and courgettes. A metal colander can be used as a steamer in the same way that a sieve can.*

KITCHEN SCALES: *these might seem essential, but tablespoons can often be used instead, and the wrappers on packs of butter and other solid fats are usually marked in portions of 25 g (1 oz). As a rough guide, each of the following level tablespoon measures is approximately equal to 25 g (1 oz): 2 tablespoons flour, 2 tablespoons rice, 2 tablespoons sugar, 2 tablespoons dried fruit, 3 tablespoons grated cheese, 2 tablespoons soft butter, and 1 tablespoons syrup, treacle or jam. However, if you do a lot of baking, for which accurate measuring is essential, you might like to invest in some scales.*

KITCHEN SCISSORS: *a large, sturdy pair of scissors is very useful for snipping rinds off bacon, chopping chives and many other things.*

KITCHEN STATIONERY: *or, in other words, clingfilm, foil, greaseproof paper and kitchen paper.*

KNIFE SHARPENER

MEASURING JUG: *if you haven't got a measuring jug, use empty milk bottles or cartons, ½-pint beer glasses, empty cream and yogurt pots, etc., for measuring liquid ingredients.*

MEASURING SPOONS: *you can buy sets of plastic measuring spoons (quite cheaply). Although useful, measuring spoons are really only essential for baking. You can use your everyday teaspoons and tablespoons for measuring ingredients in other recipes.*

OVENPROOF BAKING DISHES (GRATIN DISHES): *as well as being used as baking dishes, these can double as serving dishes. A flameproof baking dish, that is one that can be used on gas or electric rings as well as in the oven, is useful. Flameproof dishes are automatically ovenproof, but not vice versa.*

PEPPER-MILL: *whole peppercorns keep their aroma much better than ready-ground pepper, but you'll need a pepper-mill to grind them.*

ROASTING TIN: *for roasting, obviously, but also for making larger quantities of baked dishes, such as fruit crumbles.*

SPATULAS: *plastic or rubber spatulas are useful for scraping mixtures out of bowls; wooden spatulas can be used for stirring or turning foods while frying.*

VEGETABLE BRUSH: *for scrubbing potatoes and other vegetables. I use a cheap nail brush.*

VEGETABLE PEELER: *also useful for paring the zest off citrus fruit.*

WHISKS: *a small hand-held balloon whisk is great for whisking one or two egg whites or a small carton of cream, but for larger quantities a rotary whisk is easier on the arm muscles. Hand-held electric mixers are more expensive but make whisking a doddle. Some of the recipes in this book can't be made without a whisk of some sort.*

USEFUL ITEMS WORTH SAVING FOR, OR RECEIVING AS PRESENTS

BISCUIT CUTTERS: *these are very useful if you do a lot of baking, but you can use the rim of a glass or cup instead.*

CAKE TINS: *buy tins of various shapes and sizes with removable bases to make turning out cakes much easier.*

ELECTRIC BLENDERS: *small hand-held blenders are useful for liquidising or puréeing small amounts of food, and are not very expensive. For larger quantities, a free-standing blender is better, but more expensive.*

FOOD MILL: *sometimes called a mouli or mouli-légumes, this is for puréeing vegetables and soups. Food mills can be bought from most good kitchen shops and come with three discs – fine, medium and coarse – so you can choose the texture you prefer or that is appropriate for the dish you are making. Food mills are also good for making mashed potato and fruit fools.*

GARLIC PRESS: *garlic cloves can be crushed with a knife blade, but a garlic press makes the job much easier.*

PALETTE KNIFE: *this is the perfect tool for flipping over pancakes and spreading icing on cakes.*

PASTRY BRUSH

POTATO MASHER

RAMEKINS: *these are one-portion, straight-sided, ovenproof china bowl or 'pots'.*

ROLLING PIN: *but you can improvise with a clean milk bottle!*

SALAD SPINNER: *for drying lettuce and other salad leaves thoroughly.*

SKEWERS: *for kebabs, and for testing cakes and vegetables to see if they are cooked.*

SOUFFLÉ DISH: *a straight-sided, ovenproof china dish, useful as a serving dish as well as for baking.*

TART OR FLAN TINS: *buy metal tart or flan tins, not china ones which will leave pastry soggy.*

TIERED STEAMER: *either a metal steamer that can be placed straight over the heat, or Chinese bamboo steamers that sit in a saucepan or wok. Can be used to cook two or three different vegetables, or even a whole meal, over one ring.*

TONGS: *for turning things over on the grill or in the frying-pan.*

WIRE RACK: *for cooling cakes and biscuits.*

WOK: *if you like the taste of stir-fried foods, then a wok makes it much easier to cook them. Woks are not very expensive, but they do take up a lot of room in the cupboard. A large frying-pan can be used instead.*

THE STORECUPBOARD

When you are on a tight budget, it pays to plan ahead a week at a time. You may have to cut down on meat and ready-made meals, but these can be replaced with more fresh vegetables and fruit, and you can fill up with big helpings of starchy foods such as potatoes, pulses, rice, brown bread and pasta. This way you'll be eating a much healthier diet, saving money, and maybe even enjoying your meals more than before!

Even when you are only cooking for one or two people, don't ignore recipes for four. They may work out cheaper if they can be reheated or eaten cold next day. One big shopping spree each week or so is an excellent idea for stocking up on items that will keep, but fish, meat, poultry, most vegetables and fruit are best bought in smaller quantities as and when you need them.

A well-stocked storecupboard makes daily cooking a much simpler affair. Exactly what goes into the cupboard depends on your personal taste, but there are some items that no kitchen should be without. Remember to check the 'best before' dates of anything you are keeping for a while.

HEALTH AND NUTRITION

Good health is important if you want to get the most out of life, and good health starts with a healthy diet. The media bombard us with confusing information about diet, but don't panic – you don't need a degree in nutrition to get it right, nor do you have to give up every-thing you like most and live on rabbit food.

The key to a healthy diet is variety and balance. Hamburgers, pizzas and chocolate alone will not supply your body with all the vitamins and minerals it needs to function at full tilt. The more different kinds of food you eat, the more

BEANS AND OTHER PULSES, CANNED: *these are a wonderful standby. Canned kidney beans, borlotti beans, chick-peas, etc., can be used to make snappy salads, can be added to sauces and casseroles to eke them out, or they can even be mashed to make quick dips.*

BEANS AND OTHER PULSES, DRIED: *dried beans and other pulses are much cheaper than canned. However, apart from lentils and a couple of others, they do have to be soaked and cooked for some time. They are high in protein and fibre, and they taste delicious. Store in airtight containers: they keep for several months.*

CANNED TOMATOES, WHOLE AND/OR CHOPPED: *these are great for soups, stews, etc., and for quick sauces for pasta.*

CHEESE: *a hunk of cheese is worth keeping to hand for sandwiches, grating over soups, pasta or omelettes, cheese on toast, etc. Store in the warmest part of the fridge (the top shelf, unless there's an ice-making compartment, which makes the area under it cold).*

DRIED HERBS: *essential storecupboard herbs are dried thyme, sage, rosemary and bay leaves. Dried mint, marjoram and/or oregano, dill and tarragon can all be useful.*

EGGS: *always keep a few eggs handy for quick suppers – omelettes, scrambled eggs on toast, even soufflés. Keep them in a cool place or the fridge and check the 'use by' date carefully.*

FLOUR: *plain flour is essential, but if you enjoy baking, then you'll need self-raising as well. Store in a cool, dry place and use within a few months.*

OIL: *sunflower or vegetable oils are good neutral-flavoured all-rounders, not only for frying, but also for salad dressings, marinades, brushing over foods that are to be grilled, etc. Olive oil is more expensive but has the most delicious flavour in cooking. I'd opt for olive oil if I couldn't have both. Store oils in a cool, dark cupboard and use within a few months of opening.*

ONIONS AND GARLIC: *since onions and garlic are used in the vast majority of savoury dishes for background flavour, it makes sense always to keep some handy. They keep best in a cool, dark place with a clear circulation of air around them.*

PASTA, DRIED: *after eggs, the best convenience food on the market. Buy pasta in small quantities, and once the packet has been opened, store in a cool, dry place, preferably in an airtight container.*

RICE: *brown or white, rice is an excellent standby food, both as an accompaniment to other dishes and as the basis for a dish in its own right. Store in a cool, dry place, preferably in an airtight container.*

SALT AND PEPPER: *to keep salt free-flowing in a badly ventilated or damp kitchen, add a spoonful of uncooked rice to the jar to absorb moisture. If possible, buy a pepper-mill and refill regularly with dried black peppercorns.*

SPICES: *to get the best flavour from spices, buy them whole and grind them yourself with a pestle and mortar or in a strong bowl with the end of a rolling pin. Otherwise, buy ready-ground spices and use them up quickly. Make sure you have cinnamon and nutmeg, preferably a whole one which you can grate. Personally, I wouldn't be without chilli powder, cumin and coriander. Store spices in a cool, dark place, if possible.*

SUGAR: *if you intend to make puddings and cakes, then buy caster sugar which will be fine for tea and coffee as well. Granulated sugar has larger crystals which are less suitable for cooking. Keep in a cool, dry place.*

TOMATO PURÉE: *boosts the flavour of any tomatoey soup, stew, sauce, etc., and can be added to a white sauce and marinades for flavour. Unless you want to use a large quantity all at once, buy in a tube, rather than a can, so that it can be resealed. Once opened, keep the tube in the refrigerator.*

VINEGAR: *malt vinegar is a bit harsh for a lot of culinary purposes – cider or wine vinegars are better all-rounders.*

essential nutrients your body gets. At the same time, reduce your intake of fats (particularly animal or 'saturated' fats such as in butter, cream and cheese, etc.) and sugar. Aim to follow these guidelines for a healthy balanced diet that is easy to keep to:

• Eat loads of fresh fruit and vegetables, raw or cooked. You should aim for a minimum of about 400 g (1 lb) a day, excluding potatoes, and try to include pulses, nuts and seeds.

• Eat your fill of bread, potatoes and cereals, including pasta and breakfast cereals, but go easy on added butter or sugar.

• Fish, chicken and turkey are relatively low in fats so eat them frequently. Red meat and dairy products, including eggs, are good sources of protein and other nutrients, but they also contain more fat, so cut down on these. You don't need to eat meat every day, and when you do, trim off excess fat and serve smaller portions accompanied by plenty of vegetables and pulses.

VEGETARIANS

The decision to turn vegetarian should not be taken lightly. Meat provides essential proteins and other nutrients, and if you are going to cut meat out of your diet altogether, you need to know how to replace these nutrients properly. This book includes plenty of vegetarian recipes, but you might like to buy or borrow a good basic vegetarian cookery book as well, for more information on how to balance your diet.

GLOSSARY OF
BASIC TECHNIQUES

AL DENTE: *to cook pasta, vegetables, etc., until al dente means until they are just tender to the bite, but still with a slight resistance at the centre, i.e. not boiled to a soggy mass.*

BAKE BLIND: *to bake a pastry case in the oven before filling, so that the pastry remains crisp.*

BASTE: *to spoon fat or liquid over food as it cooks, usually in the oven, to keep it moist.*

BRAISE: *to stew food – usually meat on a bed of vegetables – slowly.*

BROWN OR SEAR: *to fry meat or fish briskly in fat in order to brown the outside.*

CREAM: *to beat softened butter, sometimes with sugar, until soft and creamy.*

DICE: *to cut into small cubes.*

FOLD IN: *to mix whisked egg whites or cream carefully into another mixture without breaking down all the bubbles of trapped air. Always use a large metal spoon, sliding it through the mixture, lifting and turning, rather than stirring or beating vigorously.*

MARINATE: *to leave meat, fish or vegetables in a flavoured marinade, (i.e. a mixture of spices or herbs, finely diced vegetables and liquids such as lemon juice or vinegar, and oil) for a length of time so that they absorb some of the flavour.*

POACH: *to cook food (usually eggs or fish) gently in liquid that is heated to just below simmering point. The surface of the water should merely tremble; the water should never be allowed to bubble.*

REHEAT: *to heat up food for eating that has been cooked some time earlier. When reheating foods, make sure you do it thoroughly to kill off any dangerous bacteria. Many sauces*

and most stews can be reheated in a saucepan on the hob or in an oven, but you'll probably have to add a little extra water to keep them liquid enough. Bring back to the boil, then reduce the heat and simmer for a good 5 minutes. Solid lumps of food should be reheated in the oven, protected by a sheet of foil. Timing depends on the size, but allow at least 15 minutes Gas Mark 5/190°C/ 375°F for small portions, and a minimum of 30 minutes at Gas Mark 4/180°C/350°F for larger items. Either way, double check that the centre of the food is really piping hot before eating.

RUB IN: *to mix fat into flour and other dry powdery ingredients. The chilled fat should be cut roughly into chunks, then literally rubbed into the flour between the tips of your fingers and thumbs, until the mixture resembles fine breadcrumbs.*

SIMMER: *to cook food in simmering water, i.e. in water just below boiling point. There should be a few small bubbles rising to the surface, but the water should never reach a lively rolling boil.*

STEAM: *to cook in the heat of steam alone – the best method of cooking most vegetables, and excellent for fish or chicken. If you don't have a proper steamer, you can rig up a makeshift one by setting a metal sieve or colander over a pan of boiling water, making sure that the sieve doesn't come into contact with the water. Put the food in the sieve, in as thin a layer as possible, and cover tightly.*

STIR-FRY: *a wonderful Oriental method of cooking foods quickly in hot oil. The theory is simple: foods are stirred and tossed constantly in a little hot oil in a wok or large frying-pan over a high heat, until patched with brown. When cooked, vegetables should be tender but still retain a*

small amount of crunchiness. However, there are certain guidelines to be followed:

● *Vegetables and meat should be cut into small pieces, all of much the same dimensions, so that they cook quickly and evenly.*

● *All ingredients must be prepared, measured and assembled before you start cooking.*

● *If possible, use a wok, but failing that a large, high-sided frying-pan.*

● *The secret of stir-frying is to keep the heat very high throughout the cooking period (unless the recipe says otherwise), and to keep all the ingredients constantly on the move so that they never have a chance to burn. This means that the wok/pan gets very hot indeed, so take great care not to burn yourself.*

WHISK/WHIP: *generally speaking, egg whites are whisked, cream is whipped, but the process is the same. The idea is to get as much air into the whites or cream as possible by beating very vigorously, so that they puff up in volume, stiffen and hold their shape. You can use a fork, but it's hard work. A wire balloon whisk or a rotary beater is a much better option, and will give greater volume in the end.*

Whip double or whipping cream (but not single) until it just holds its shape, but don't overdo it or you'll end up with butter. Stiffly whisked egg whites will remain in stiff peaks when the whisk is pulled up out of the bowl. When a recipe tells you to whisk to soft peaks, the tips of the peaks should flop over when the whisk is lifted out. Always use whisked egg whites straight away before they collapse to a puddle.

SOUPS AND SAUCES

Home-made soups taste very different from canned soups, and you can make a soup to fit any occasion. I really enjoy making soup of practically any kind. Soup-making, by and large, is not a complicated business, and it is a very satisfying process. Once you get the gist of the basic methods, you'll find that you can make any number of variations on a simple theme.

The serving quantities given in the following recipes are deliberately vague. For a first course, a small bowlful is usually adequate: a big bowlful is the order of the day if it's the mainstay of your meal.

Soup can be snappily jazzed up with last-minute extras that provide contrasting crunch or flavour. Stir in a generous spoonful of cream or yogurt just before serving, or sprinkle bowls of soup with chopped fresh herbs, crumbled crisply-grilled bacon, grated cheese or cubes of crisply fried bread (*croûtons*). To make a soup more substantial, float pieces of freshly made cheese on toast (cheese *croûtes*), made with French bread and grated Cheddar or Gruyère cheese, on top of each bowlful.

Simple sauces and salad dressings make all the difference, transforming plain foods into interesting dishes in the twinkling of an eye. Imagine that you've just got home, a little tired and very hungry. Supper is on your mind – something to fill the yawning gap in your stomach and to perk you up after a busy day, something that won't take too long to cook but will satisfy your taste-buds. You look in the fridge and find a couple of sausages, a potato or two, a few lettuce leaves and half a cucumber. Hmm, the basic menu is quick enough to throw together but not exactly exciting – grilled sausages, boiled potatoes and a worthy but dull salad.

However, if you also happen to have a few basic supplies stashed away for just such an occasion, you can transform the menu into something a lot more worthwhile in just 5 minutes extra in the kitchen. Add a can of tomatoes, an onion, garlic, oil, vinegar and mustard and the menu now reads 'sausages *à l'italienne*' (i.e. with a garlicky tomato sauce), either boiled potatoes or a hot potato salad, and a mixed green salad with French dressing'. Now that is a lot more likely to hit the spot than menu number one.

It is easy to make soups and sauces in large quantities, simply by increasing the amount of ingredients.

CHUNKY TOMATO SOUP

Preparation time: 10 minutes + 25 minutes cooking   Serves 3–4

1 tablespoon olive or sunflower oil	Heat the oil in a saucepan large enough to hold all the ingredients. Add the onion, garlic, carrot, bay leaf, thyme and parsley. Stir, then cover and turn the heat down very low. Cook for 10 minutes, stirring once or twice, then add all the remaining ingredients. Bring to the boil then reduce the heat and simmer for 15 minutes. Remove the bay leaf and parsley sprigs, taste the soup and generously adjust the seasoning. To garnish with basil or chives, scatter them over the top of the soup just before serving. If using double cream, take the hot soup off the heat, and stir it in just before serving.
1 onion, chopped	
2 garlic cloves, chopped	
1 carrot, chopped finely	
1 bay leaf	
½ teaspoon dried thyme	
2 sprigs of fresh parsley	
397 g (14 oz) can of chopped tomatoes	
1 tablespoon tomato purée	*Smooth Tomato Soup:* Make a chunky tomato soup, liquidise, and sieve. Reheat and garnish as above.
1 teaspoon sugar	
450 ml (¾ pint) vegetable or chicken stock, or water	
salt and pepper	

To garnish:

8 large fresh basil leaves, roughly torn up, or 2 tablespoons finely chopped fresh chives, or 142 ml (5 fl oz) carton of double cream (optional)

SPLIT PEA SOUP

Preparation time: 20 minutes + soaking + 1 hour cooking   Serves 6

375 g (12 oz) split green or yellow peas, soaked for at least 4 hours

2 large carrots, chopped finely

1 large onion, chopped

2 celery sticks, chopped finely

2 garlic cloves, crushed

1 bay leaf

1 sprig of fresh thyme, or ½ teaspoon dried thyme

3 sprigs of fresh parsley

1.5 litres (2½ pints) chicken or vegetable stock, or water

salt and pepper

6 tablespoons thick greek-style yogurt, to serve

This is a good, satisfying old-fashioned soup, perfect for a cold winter's night. Dried split peas, green or yellow, collapse naturally to make a thick purée so you won't need a blender, though if you do have one, the soup can be puréed to smooth out the chunks of vegetable.

Drain the split peas and put them in a large saucepan with all the vegetables and herbs. Season with salt and pepper and add enough stock or water to cover by about 2.5 cm (1 inch). Bring to the boil and boil rapidly for 10 minutes, then reduce the heat and simmer gently for about 1-1½ hours or until the peas have collapsed to a rough purée (you can help them along by crushing them against the side of the pan with the back of a spoon). Stir occasionally to prevent the soup sticking on the bottom of the pan, and add extra water if the soup gets too thick. Taste and adjust the seasoning. Remove the bay leaf and thyme and parsley sprigs. Serve piping hot, with a tablespoon of thick yogurt added to each bowl.

Split Pea Soup

Cod Chowder

Chunky Tomato Soup

COD CHOWDER

Preparation time: 35 minutes + 20 minutes cooking   Serves 6

50 g (2 oz) butter

1 large onion, chopped

250 g (8 oz) smoked back bacon, de-rinded and cut into 1 cm (½-inch) wide strips

500 g (1 lb) carrots, cut into 1 cm (½-inch) lengths

5 celery sticks, cut into 1 cm (½-inch) lengths

2 green peppers, de-seeded and chopped

500 g (1 lb) potatoes, cut into 1 cm (½-inch) cubes

50 g (2 oz) plain flour

1 bay leaf

2 tablespoons chopped fresh parsley

2 sprigs of fresh thyme

1.2 litres (2 pints) milk, or 600 ml (1 pint) milk and 600 ml (1 pint) fish stock

500 g (1 lb) fresh cod fillet or lightly smoked cod, cut into 2.5 cm (1-inch) cubes

salt and pepper

grated Cheddar cheese, to serve

I started making chowders when I was a student. In the early part of the term, I could afford a nice chunk of cod to go into the soup, but towards the end of term, when my grant was running low if it still existed at all, the fish disappeared and I made pure vegetable chowders.

Melt the butter in a saucepan large enough to hold all the ingredients. Add the onion and bacon, and fry gently until tender but not brown. Add all the vegetables and stir to coat evenly with butter. Sprinkle in the flour and stir for 1 minute to distribute it evenly. Add the herbs, then the milk, or milk and stock if using. Season lightly with pepper and bring to the boil. Reduce the heat and simmer gently for 15–20 minutes or until the vegetables are just cooked, stirring occasionally to make sure the soup doesn't catch on the bottom of the pan. Add the cod, continue to simmer for 2–3 minutes more or until the fish is just cooked. Taste and adjust the seasoning, adding salt only if necessary. Fish out the thyme sprigs (if you can find them) and serve with grated cheese.

CHUNKY TOMATO SAUCE

Preparation and cooking time: 20–30 minutes
Serves 2–3 with pasta, or 4 as a sauce with meat

1 tablespoon olive or sunflower oil

This is one of the easiest and most useful sauces ever. It's great on pasta with grated cheese and perks up plain grilled pork chops or hamburgers. Once you've

1 onion, chopped

1 large or 2 small garlic cloves, chopped

2 sprigs of fresh thyme, or ½ teaspoon dried thyme

400 g (14 oz) can of tomatoes, or 500 g (1 lb) fresh tomatoes, skinned and roughly chopped

1 tablespoon tomato purée

½ teaspoon caster sugar

salt and pepper

mastered the knack of making the basic sauce, you can start to explore its endless variations, a few of which I've given below. The sauce can be made up to 48 hours in advance and reheated when you need it. When cool, cover it and keep it in the fridge. Since it keeps so well, it may be worth making double or treble the quantity.

Heat the oil in a pan over a fairly low heat. Add the onion and garlic, and cook gently until tender but not brown, stirring occasionally. (If they start to brown, turn the heat down a little.)

Add the remaining ingredients and turn the heat up. Once the sauce is bubbling, stir it occasionally, crushing the tomatoes with the spoon. Cook for 5–15 minutes or until the sauce is thick, with no trace of wateriness. (The cooking time will depend on the width of the pan you are using; a wider pan will allow the liquid to evaporate more quickly.) Taste and adjust the seasoning, adding a little more sugar if the sauce is on the sharp side. If you use fresh thyme remove the sprigs before serving the sauce.

Variations: For a less chunky tomato sauce, use a 397 g (14 oz) can of chopped tomatoes instead of whole tomatoes. For a smooth sauce, leave it to cool slightly, then pass it through the fine blades of a food mill or purée until smooth in a blender or food processor. If you don't have any of these, push the sauce through a sieve. Reheat when needed. **Tomato and Basil Sauce** Stir in 8–12 roughly chopped fresh basil leaves before serving. **Tomato and Orange Sauce** Add the juice of 1 orange at the same time as you add the tomatoes. **Tomato, Chilli and Ginger Sauce** Omit the thyme. At the same time as you add the onion and garlic, add 1 de-seeded and chopped fresh chilli, or ¼ teaspoon chilli powder, and 1 cm (½-inch) piece of fresh root ginger, peeled and finely chopped. Serve with grilled chicken or fish. **Creamy Tomato Sauce** Sieve or purée the sauce until smooth. Return the sauce to the pan and stir in a 142 ml (5 fl oz) carton of whipping or double cream.

19

Bring gently to the boil, then reduce the heat and simmer for 2 minutes. Taste and adjust the seasoning before serving with grilled steak, roast chicken or pasta. (This serves 5–6 people.)

Tomato Sauce à l'Italienne Increase the quantity of garlic to 3 or even 4 cloves.

BASIC WHITE SAUCE

Preparation and cooking time: 12 minutes   Makes about 300 ml (½ pint)

25 g (1 oz) butter

25 g (1 oz) plain flour

300 ml (½ pint) milk

salt, pepper and freshly grated or ground nutmeg

Making a smooth white sauce is easy, as long as you don't rush it when you begin to add the milk. A white sauce is used in many dishes, so it really is worth mastering the technique.

Melt the butter in a saucepan, stir in the flour and continue stirring over a low heat for 1 minute. Remove from the heat and gradually add the milk, a little at a time, mixing it in well. Once you've reached the stage when the sauce has become a smooth, thick liquid, start increasing the quantity of milk you add each time, stirring until it is all incorporated.

Return the pan to the heat, bring the sauce slowly to the boil, stirring constantly, and simmer gently for 5 minutes, stirring frequently to prevent sticking. Season with salt and pepper, and add nutmeg to taste.

Variations: **Cheese Sauce** Before seasoning, remove the sauce from the heat and stir in about 50 g (2 oz) grated Cheddar cheese, adding it gradually and tasting as you go until you have a strong enough flavour. Season with salt and pepper.

Note: If you make the sauce in advance, spear a knob of butter on the tip of a knife and rub it over the surface of the sauce before cooling. This prevents a skin forming on the surface.

CHEESE AND EGGS

The egg is nature's convenience food. Each one arrives in its own neat, one-portion package and has a hundred and one potential uses. Eggs are packed with protein, and have a flavour that is both clear enough to stand on its own and adaptable enough to blend with whatever you care to put with it. Half a dozen eggs won't make too big a dent in your pocket, and they are quick and easy to cook. I can't think of any man-made convenience food that can compete.

Cheese and eggs are natural partners, though not all the recipes in this chapter include both. When I'm at home on my own, I often make myself a quick cheese omelette for lunch or supper. If friends ring at the last minute to invite themselves for supper, it doesn't take long to knock up Welsh Rarebit or one of the other dishes in this chapter. It's well worth keeping half a dozen eggs and a hunk of cheese in the fridge for hungry moments and last-minute visitors.

WELSH RAREBIT

Preparation and cooking time: 15 minutes — Serves 2

125 g (4 oz) mature Cheddar cheese, grated

3 tablespoons pale ale, dry white wine or milk

15 g (½ oz) butter

2 large slices of bread, toasted

mustard

pepper

chilli powder

Put the cheese and pale ale, wine or milk in a saucepan with the butter and stir over a low heat until the cheese and butter have melted and the mixture is smooth and creamy. Don't let it boil. Season with pepper. Preheat the grill to hot.

Spread the toast slices thinly with mustard and lay them side-by-side, mustard-side up, in a shallow flameproof dish which is just large enough for them. Pour over the cheese mixture and dust with a little chilli powder. Put under the grill until golden brown and bubbling. Serve immediately with a green salad.

Variation: Top the mustard-coated toast with thin slices of tomato before pouring over the cheese sauce.

CARROT AND COURGETTE CAKE

Preparation time: 45 minutes + 30 minutes cooking

Serves 5–6 as a main course, 8 as a first course

500 g (1 lb) courgettes

500 g (1 lb) carrots

leaves of 2 sprigs of fresh thyme, chopped

1 tablespoon chopped fresh parsley

25 g (1 oz) plain flour, sifted

¼ teaspoon freshly grated nutmeg, or a pinch of ground nutmeg

2 eggs, beaten

1 tablespoon olive or sunflower oil

salt and pepper

This is a great lunch or light supper dish, or it could be served as a first course or side dish, or you could even take it with you for a packed lunch. It tastes wonderful hot from the oven, at its best when warm, and almost as good cold.

Don't be tempted to speed things up by skipping the salting of the courgettes. The salt forces them to release some of their moisture, which firstly improves the flavour, and secondly leaves less moisture to ooze out in the heat of the oven, diluting the egg and flour mixture which holds the 'cake' together.

If you want to make double or treble the quantity, bake the mixture in a roasting tin large enough to give a depth of 2.5–4 cm (1–1½ inches).

Grate the courgettes coarsely, spread them in a colander and sprinkle lightly with salt. Turn to mix, then set aside for 30 minutes.

Preheat the oven to Gas Mark 5/190°C/ 375°F. Squeeze the courgettes to remove excess moisture, then put them in a bowl. Grate the carrots and squeeze out as much liquid as possible. Add the carrots to the courgettes with the herbs and mix well. Sprinkle over the flour, nutmeg and plenty of pepper and mix evenly. Stir in the eggs.

Generously oil an 18 cm (7-inch) cake tin, flan tin or baking dish. Spread the mixture evenly in the tin and drizzle the oil over the surface. Bake in the oven for 30 minutes or until browned on top. Serve hot, warm or cold, cut into wedges.

OMELETTE

Preparation and cooking time: 5–7 minutes

Serves 1

2–3 eggs, depending on appetite

15 g (½ oz) butter

salt and pepper

Anybody can make an omelette, but not everyone knows how to make a really sensational omelette. It takes practice to get it just right. The perfect omelette is light and melting, still slightly moist and creamy in the centre, while lightly browned but still tender on the outside, and not overcooked and leathery.

Happily, eggs are not expensive, so you can afford to practise until you perfect your skills. Until you become a dab hand with the omelette pan, it's best to make individual omelettes, using only two or three eggs. Always eat omelettes freshly made and still hot from the pan.

You can flavour an omelette in a variety of ways – add grated cheese, lightly fried sliced mushrooms, chopped ham or chicken, or flaked smoked fish to the omelette before folding it, or add chopped fresh herbs to the beaten egg before cooking.

Beat the eggs lightly and season well with salt and pepper. Melt the butter in a small, heavy-based frying-pan over a moderate heat, swirling it around to coat the pan evenly. As soon as the butter stops foaming, pour in the eggs.

Tilt the pan so that the egg spreads evenly. Using a palette knife or spatula, carefully lift the edges of the omelette towards the centre as they set, tilting the pan so that the unset egg can run down to fill the gaps. Continue working your way quickly around the omelette, until all the egg has just set, leaving the surface of the omelette moist and creamy but not runny.

Slip the knife or spatula under one side of the omelette and fold it over to cover the centre. Lift the other side over on top, then carefully slide the omelette on to a serving plate. Eat immediately.

23

CHEESE STRATA

Preparation time: 7 minutes + 25–30 minutes cooking   Serves 1

2 large slices of wholemeal bread

butter

mustard (optional)

25 g (1 oz) Cheddar or other cheese, grated

150 ml (¼ pint) milk

1 egg, beaten

½ tablespoon chopped fresh parsley (optional)

salt and pepper

This is a savoury version of bread and butter pudding, and is a quick way to turn an ordinary sandwich into a main course. You can adapt the idea to make other kinds of Strata, perhaps adding a few slices of tomato, or using ham or prawns instead of cheese.

Preheat the oven to Gas Mark 4/180°C/350°F. Spread the bread thinly with butter, then with a little mustard, if using. Cut off the crusts, and use the bread slices and cheese to make a sandwich. Cut the sandwich into quarters and pack tightly, overlapping slightly, into a small (about 15 cm/6-inch diameter), lightly buttered ovenproof dish.

Beat the milk with the egg and parsley, if using. Season with salt and pepper, and pour over the sandwich. Bake for 25–30 minutes or until the custard is just set and the upper layer of bread is lightly browned.

Cheese Strata

Glamorgan Sausages

Omelette, with mushrooms

GLAMORGAN SAUSAGES

Preparation and cooking time: 35 minutes   Serves 4

175–200 g (6–7 oz) fresh white breadcrumbs

150 g (5 oz) Caerphilly cheese or mild vegetarian cheese, crumbled or grated

½ leek, very finely chopped

1 tablespoon chopped fresh parsley

¼ teaspoon dried thyme

2 eggs, beaten

1½ teaspoons English mustard, or 2 teaspoons Dijon mustard

2–3 tablespoons milk

40 g (1½ oz) butter or 3 tablespoons oil for frying or grilling

salt and pepper

Despite their name, Glamorgan sausages have absolutely no meat in them, so they are ideal for vegetarians and meat-eaters alike. The 'sausages' can be prepared up to a day in advance, then cooked when needed. Breadcrumbs can be made quickly in a blender or food processor, but if you haven't got one, tear the bread apart with your hands.

Put 150 g (5 oz) of the breadcrumbs in a bowl and add the cheese, leek, parsley, thyme and plenty of salt and pepper. Mix well. Beat the eggs with the mustard. Set aside 2 tablespoons of the egg mixture, and stir the remainder into the crumbs and cheese, adding just enough milk to bind the mixture together without making it sloppy.

Divide the mixture into eight and shape into sausages, about 2.5 cm (1 inch) in diameter. Put the reserved egg and mustard mixture in a shallow bowl, and put the remaining bread-crumbs on a plate. Dip each sausage in the egg, then roll in the crumbs until evenly coated. If you have time, chill the sausages in the fridge for 30 minutes or until firm. (They can be kept in the fridge for up to 24 hours.)

Heat the butter or oil in a frying-pan and fry the sausages briskly for about 5 minutes or until brown, then lower the heat for a final 3–4 minutes to cook through. Alternatively, brush the sausages with oil or melted butter and cook them under a preheated grill for about 10 minutes or until well browned on all sides, turning them every 1–2 minutes.

PASTA, RICE AND PULSES

Pasta is one of the all-time great convenience foods. It is cheap, quick to cook, keeps well, tastes good and can be served in a hundred-and-one different ways. What more can you ask for? I always keep a packet of spaghetti, tagliatelle or fusilli in the cupboard, ready to make a quick pasta meal which might be as simple as plain pasta with a splash of olive oil, some crushed garlic and plenty of grated cheese.

Rice is another store-cupboard treasure and one that's not always used to its full potential. If you thought rice was just something to dish up alongside Indian and Chinese food, then you've been missing out. Plain-cooked rice is good with practically any dish that has plenty of sauce, and it plays a more major role in dishes such as risottos and pilaus. Follow packet instructions for cooking rice and pasta.

There's a huge range of pulses, and a wealth of ways to prepare them. Quite apart from the fact that they taste good, they are cheap and filling and positively good for you. You can buy all of them dried, and many of them canned.

You'll save money by buying packets of dried pulses, though most of them will need overnight soaking before they can be cooked. Canned beans are more expensive, but are ready to be used straight away. Follow packet instructions for soaking and cooking dried pulses, and remember always to boil them fast for 10 minutes, to get rid of the toxins that are in some raw beans, especially red kidney beans.

PASTA WITH BROCCOLI, HAM AND GRUYÈRE

Preparation and cooking time: 15 minutes   Serves 4

500 g (1 lb) broccoli

500 g (1 lb) tagliatelle

50 g (2 oz) butter

1 small onion, chopped

3 thick slices of cooked ham, cut into strips

125 g (4 oz) Gruyère cheese, grated

freshly grated nutmeg

salt and pepper

Pasta with broccoli is popular in southern Italy. This recipe stretches the idea a step further by adding ham and Gruyère cheese. You might like to adapt it by replacing the ham with 125 g (4 oz) sliced mushrooms cooked with the onion and a little extra butter.

Separate the broccoli into small florets and slice the stems thinly. Bring a large saucepan of lightly salted water to the boil and add the broccoli, tagliatelle and 15 g (½ oz) butter. Bring back to the boil, then reduce the heat and simmer for 10–12 minutes or until the tagliatelle is *al dente* (tender but with a slight bite to it).

Meanwhile, heat 25 g (1 oz) of the remaining butter in a frying-pan, add the onion and fry until soft but not brown. Add the ham and cook for a further 1–2 minutes. Turn the heat down low and keep warm.

When the pasta is cooked, drain it and immediately return it to the hot saucepan. Mix in the onion and ham and the remaining butter, and season with nutmeg, salt and pepper. Pile the pasta into a warmed serving dish and sprinkle with half the cheese. Serve immediately, with the remaining cheese for those who want it.

Pasta with Broccoli, Ham and Gruyère

Fusilli with Courgettes

Jambalaya

JAMBALAYA

Preparation time: 40 minutes + 25 minutes cooking   Serves 6

375 g (12 oz) streaky pork rashers, cut into small pieces

25 g (1 oz) butter

1 onion, chopped

3 celery sticks, sliced thinly

1 red pepper, de-seeded and chopped

375 g (12 oz) long-grain rice

2 sprigs of fresh thyme, or 1 teaspoon dried thyme

1 bay leaf

1½ × 397 g (14 oz) can of chopped tomatoes

2 teaspoons caster sugar

900 ml (1½ pints) hot water

4 spring onions, chopped roughly

125 g (4 oz) peeled cooked prawns

2 tablespoons chopped fresh parsley

Tabasco sauce

salt and pepper

Jambalaya is a big exuberant medley of ingredients. There's rice, there's pork, there's prawns, there's tomatoes and vegetables, and they all come together to make a wonderful filling meal.

Put the pork in a large saucepan and fry until brown, starting off over a medium-low heat and raising the heat as the fat begins to run. Scoop the pork out, leaving the fat behind.

Add the butter to the pan, and when it has melted, add the onion, celery and red pepper. Cook gently over a low heat until the onion is tender but not brown.

Add the rice, thyme and bay leaf to the pan and stir for 1 minute. Finally, return the pork to the pan with the canned tomatoes and sugar. Season with salt and pepper and add the hot water. Bring gently to the boil, then reduce the heat and simmer very slowly for 25 minutes or until the rice is cooked and most of the liquid has been absorbed. Stir occasionally to prevent the mixture catching on the bottom of the pan, and add a little extra water, if necessary.

When the rice is cooked, stir in the spring onions, prawns and parsley. Add Tabasco sauce to taste. (Go easy at first as it is fairly punchy – start with ½ teaspoon and add more if you like things hot.) Taste and add extra salt if needed. Serve hot.

FUSILLI WITH COURGETTES

Preparation and cooking time: 45 minutes   Serves 2

250 g (8 oz) fusilli or other pasta shapes

1 tablespoon olive oil

freshly grated parmesan or Cheddar cheese, to serve

For the sauce:

2 courgettes (about 250 g/8 oz) cut into 5 mm (¼-inch) cubes

2 tablespoons olive oil

1 small onion, chopped

2 garlic cloves, chopped

1 tablespoon chopped fresh parsley

salt and pepper

I make this pasta dish for myself time and time again. Little cubes of courgettes are fried until they turn wonderfully brown and melting, then are tossed with fusilli or other pasta shapes. Don't skip the salting of the courgettes, which draws out some of their moisture and concentrates the flavour.

Put the courgettes in a colander and sprinkle with 1 teaspoon salt. Turn to coat, then leave to drain for 30 minutes. Rinse and pat dry on kitchen paper.

Put a large pan of lightly salted water on to boil. When it is almost boiling, start making the sauce. Heat the oil in a frying-pan, add the onion and garlic and cook gently until tender but not brown. Raise the heat, add the courgettes and fry, stirring, for 6–8 minutes or until they are patched with brown and the onion and garlic are a rich brown. Season with salt and pepper.

As soon as the water boils, add the fusilli. Follow the packet instructions and cook for 10–12 minutes or until just *al dente* (tender but with a slight bite to it). Drain well, and toss with the olive oil. Turn the pasta into a warmed bowl and keep warm if the courgettes aren't quite done yet. Spoon the courgettes and onion over the pasta, stir in the parsley and serve with grated cheese.

TIBETAN FRIED NOODLES

Preparation and cooking time: 25–30 minutes   Serves 2

175 g (6 oz) Chinese egg noodles

15 g (½ oz) butter

1 tablespoon vegetable oil

½ red onion, sliced

1 garlic clove, crushed

125 g (4 oz) boneless lamb, cut into 1 cm (½-inch) cubes

1 cm (½-inch) piece of fresh root ginger, peeled and grated

75 g (3 oz) finely shredded white cabbage

1½ tablespoons soy sauce

2 tomatoes, de-seeded and chopped roughly

3 spring onions, chopped

salt and pepper

chilli sauce, to serve (optional)

I was given this for lunch in a Tibetan village in eastern India. It was so good that I often make it for a quick lunch or supper at home. It uses quick-cooking Chinese egg noodles which are sold in flat slabs. Boneless lamb chops are an ideal cut for this. If stir-frying is an unfamiliar technique, read the notes in the Glossary of Basic Techniques in the introduction before getting out the wok or frying-pan.

Follow the packet instructions and cook the noodles in boiling salted water until tender. Drain thoroughly, then mix with the butter.

Heat the oil in a large frying-pan or wok over a high heat and add the red onion and garlic. Stir-fry over a high heat for 2–3 minutes until tender and lightly browned. Add the lamb, ginger and cabbage and stir-fry for 1–2 minutes or until the meat is just cooked. Add the soy sauce and stir-fry for a further 1–2 minutes. Add the noodles and tomatoes, and season with a little salt. Toss and turn over a high heat until evenly mixed and piping hot. Scatter with chopped spring onions and serve at once, offering chilli sauce on the side for those who want it.

Keema Pilau (Minced Meat Pilau)
Tibetan Fried Noodles

KEEMA PILAU (MINCED MEAT PILAU)

Preparation time: 20 minutes + 15–20 minutes cooking   Serves 4

250 g (8 oz) basmati or long-grain rice

25 g (1 oz) butter

1 tablespoon oil

1 onion, chopped

2 garlic cloves, chopped finely

The addition of minced beef and broad beans (you can substitute peas if you don't like broad beans) turns this pilau into a main course dish, delicious topped with a dollop of yogurt.

Put the rice in a sieve and rinse under cold water. Leave to drain while cooking the onion and minced meat.

Melt the butter with the oil in a saucepan, add the onion and garlic, and fry until the onion is

250 g (8 oz) minced beef or lamb

1 teaspoon cumin seeds

3 cloves

1–2 teaspoons ground turmeric

600 ml (1 pint) water

175 g (6 oz) frozen broad beans, thawed

salt and pepper

150 g (5 oz) carton of natural yogurt, to serve

tender but not brown. Raise the heat a little and add the minced beef or lamb. Fry, breaking up the lumps with a spoon, until the meat is no longer red. Add the spices and 150 ml (¼ pint) of the water and bring to the boil, then reduce the heat and simmer gently until most of the water has evaporated.

Stir the rice, beans and remaining water into the meat, season, raise the heat and bring to the boil. Turn the heat down as low as possible, cover the pan tightly and cook for 15–20 minutes or until all the water has been absorbed and the rice is tender. Check occasionally towards the end of the cooking time to make sure it has not boiled dry. Serve immediately, with the yogurt.

Pictured on the front cover.

LENTILS PROVENÇALE

Preparation and cooking time: 30 minutes   Serves 4–6

375 g (12 oz) brown or green lentils

½ teaspoon dried thyme

1 onion, quartered

2 tablespoons olive or sunflower oil

1 onion, chopped

2 garlic cloves, chopped

375 g (12 oz) tomatoes, skinned, de-seeded and chopped

2 tablespoons chopped fresh parsley

salt and pepper

Hot cooked lentils make an excellent accompaniment to grilled sausages and meats. Leftovers are good cold, or can be puréed and reheated with a knob of butter.

Put the lentils in a large saucepan with the thyme and quartered onion, and pour in enough water to cover by about 5 cm (2 inches). Bring to the boil, then reduce the heat and simmer for 15–30 minutes or until the lentils are just tender, but not collapsing.

Meanwhile, heat the oil in frying-pan and add the chopped onion and garlic. Fry over a medium-high heat until they begin to brown. Add the tomatoes and cook for a few minutes longer or until they begin to collapse.

Drain the lentils, then mix with the tomato mixture. Stir in the parsley, and season with salt and pepper. Serve hot or cold.

SPAGHETTI BOLOGNESE

Preparation time: 30 minutes + 1½ hours cooking

4 tablespoons olive or
sunflower oil

1 onion, chopped finely

1 carrot, chopped finely

1 celery stick, chopped finely

375 g (12 oz) minced beef

75 g (3 oz) unsmoked
streaky bacon, de-rinded
and chopped finely

225 ml (7 fl oz) red wine
or water

250 ml (8 fl oz) water

3 tablespoons tomato purée

1 teaspoon dried thyme

175 ml (6 fl oz) milk

500 g (1 lb) spaghetti

salt and pepper

freshly grated parmesan
cheese, to serve

*A well-made Bolognese sauce is a real treat, ... it
pays to learn how to make it properly. Make the full
quantity of sauce even if there aren't four mouths to
feed, as it tastes even better reheated a day after it is
made. As an alternative to spaghetti, serve the sauce
on baked potatoes, or with rice, topped with grated
cheese.*

Heat the oil in a large saucepan, add the onion,
carrot and celery and fry over a moderate heat
until soft and lightly browned. Add the beef and
bacon, raise the heat and cook, stirring to break
up the lumps, for 5–10 minutes or until the beef
is no longer red. If using wine, add it to the pan
with the water. If not, add 450 ml (¾ pint)
water. Stir in the tomato purée and thyme, and
season with salt and pepper. Bring to the boil,
then reduce the heat, cover and simmer over a
low heat for 1 hour, stirring occasionally. Stir in
the milk, then continue cooking, uncovered,
over a low heat, for a further 30 minutes or until
thick.

Meanwhile, bring a large saucepan of water to
the boil and slowly add the spaghetti. Follow the
packet instructions and cook for 10–12 minutes
or until the spaghetti is *al dente* (tender but with
a slight bite to it). Drain well and divide
between four bowls. Spoon the sauce over the
top and serve at once, accompanied by parmesan
cheese.

TUNA AND WHITE BEAN SALAD

Preparation time: 10 minutes + soaking and
cooking dried beans, if used   Serves 4

*432 g (15 oz) can of
cannellini beans, or 175 g
(6 oz) dried haricot beans,
soaked and cooked according
to packet instructions*

*198 g (7 oz) can of tuna,
drained and flaked*

1 garlic clove, crushed

½ red onion, chopped finely

salt and pepper

For the dressing:

1½ tablespoons lemon juice

*about 3 tablespoons olive or
sunflower oil*

*1 teaspoon chopped fresh
marjoram, or ½ teaspoon
dried oregano*

*This is a classic Italian hors d'oeuvre, and can be eked
out, by the addition of slices of tomato and hard-boiled
egg, to make a good lunch or a light supper dish.*

Rinse and drain the beans thoroughly and put in
a bowl with the tuna, garlic and onion.

Shake the dressing ingredients together in a
screw-top jar, or whisk together in a bowl, and
pour over the salad. Taste and adjust the
seasoning, adding a little more oil if it is too
sharp, and serve at room temperature.

*Lentil Salad
Tuna and White Bean Salad*

LENTIL SALAD

Preparation and cooking time: 40 minutes
+ 15–30 minutes cooking   Serves 4

*250 g (8 oz) brown or
green lentils*

1 small onion, quartered

2 whole garlic cloves

*a bouquet garni (a sprig each
of parsley, thyme and
rosemary, and a bay leaf,
tied together with string)*

1 tablespoon wine vinegar

*4 tablespoons olive or
sunflower oil*

*1 tablespoon chopped fresh
parsley*

*The key to making a good lentil salad is not to
overcook the lentils. Whip the pan off the heat as soon
as they are just tender but still firm with a nutty taste.
They can simply be dressed, while hot, with olive oil,
good wine vinegar, salt and pepper, or jazzed up as in
this recipe with extra ingredients, to be served as a
course on their own.*

Put the lentils in a large saucepan with the
onion, garlic and bouquet garni. Add enough
water to cover generously and bring gently to
the boil, then reduce the heat and simmer for
15-30 minutes or until the lentils are just tender.
Drain thoroughly, and pick out the bouquet
garni, garlic and onion. Put the lentils in a bowl

½ tablespoon chopped fresh mint

3 tomatoes, de-seeded and chopped finely

8 black olives, halved and pitted

4 hard-boiled eggs, quartered lengthways

salt and pepper

and add the vinegar, oil, parsley and mint. Season with salt and pepper and toss together, then leave to cool.

Mix the tomatoes and olives into the salad, then taste and adjust the seasoning. Just before serving, spoon into the centre of a shallow serving dish, and arrange the quartered eggs around the edge.

SPAGHETTI CARBONARA

Preparation and cooking time: 20–25 minutes   Serves 2

250 g (8 oz) spaghetti

1 tablespoon olive oil

1 garlic clove, sliced

2–3 smoked streaky bacon rashers, de-rinded and cut into thin strips

3 eggs, lightly beaten

2 tablespoons freshly grated parmesan cheese, plus extra to serve

1 tablespoon chopped fresh parsley

salt and pepper

Bring a large saucepan of lightly salted water to the boil and add the spaghetti. Follow packet instructions and cook for 10–12 minutes or until al dente (tender but with a slight bite to it). Meanwhile, heat the olive oil in a frying-pan and add the garlic. Fry gently until lightly browned, then scoop out and discard. Add the bacon to the pan and cook over a high heat for 1–2 minutes or until brown and crisp. Remove the pan from the heat and set aside until the spaghetti is almost cooked.

When the spaghetti is almost done, reheat the bacon in its oil. Drain the spaghetti, then return it immediately to the hot saucepan. Pour over the beaten egg, then the sizzling bacon and its fat. Toss well, then add the cheese and parsley. Season with salt and pepper and toss again. The heat of the spaghetti should thicken the eggs slightly to form a sauce that is still a little runny. If necessary, return the pan to the heat for a few seconds, tossing all the time, to thicken the sauce. Serve immediately, with extra parmesan.

DRY SPICED BUTTER BEANS AND CAULIFLOWER

Preparation and cooking time: 20 minutes

Serves 2 as a main dish, 3–4 as a side dish

220 g (7 oz) can of butter beans

½ cauliflower (about 175–250 g/6–8 oz)

2 teaspoons sunflower oil

1 cm (½-inch) piece of fresh root ginger, peeled and chopped finely

1 garlic clove, chopped

¼ teaspoon chilli powder

½ teaspoon ground turmeric

1 teaspoon ground cumin

1 teaspoon lemon juice

½ teaspoon garam masala (optional)

salt

Butter beans have a floury, melting texture and a gentle taste which takes well to spices. In this recipe they are combined with cauliflower to make an Indian-style vegetable dish that can be eaten as a side dish or as a vegetarian main course. Garam masala is a special spice mix that is added at the end of cooking for extra zip. It's by no means essential, so if you can't find it in your spice rack, don't worry. This recipe can be made in double quantities, but add 6 tablespoons water at first, and allow a little extra time for the cauliflower to cook.

Drain the butter beans and rinse in cold water. Break or cut the cauliflower into small florets no larger than 2.5 cm (1 inch) long and wide.

Heat the oil in a frying-pan over a medium heat. Add the ginger and garlic and fry for about 30 seconds. Add the chilli powder, turmeric and cumin, stir, then add the cauliflower and season with salt. Turn gently so that the cauliflower is coated in spices, then add 4 tablespoons water. Turn the heat down low and cover the pan tightly. Cook for 5 minutes.

Add the butter beans and lemon juice to the pan, stir to mix and cover again. Cook for a further 5 minutes or until the cauliflower is just tender, stirring once and adding more water if the mixture seems very dry. By the end of the cooking time all the liquid should have been absorbed. Stir in the garam masala, if used, and serve hot or cold.

RED BEANS AND RICE

Preparation time: 25 minutes + overnight soaking
+ 2¼ hours cooking

Serves 6

*500 g (1 lb) dried red
kidney beans, soaked
overnight*

*375 g (12 oz) smoked back
bacon, de-rinded and cut
into thick strips*

1 large onion, chopped

*1 green pepper, de-seeded
and chopped*

2 celery sticks, chopped

3 garlic cloves, chopped

1 bay leaf

*2 sprigs of fresh thyme, or
½ tablespoon dried thyme*

50 g (2 oz) butter

*3 tablespoons finely chopped
fresh parsley*

*250 g (8 oz) long-grain
white or brown rice*

salt and pepper

*Thick, creamy and hearty, this is perfect cold-weather
comfort food. There's nothing remotely elegant or
sophisticated about this dish, so just dig in and enjoy
it. The beans taste even better when reheated, so make
them a day, or even two, in advance, and store,
covered, in the fridge until you want them.*

Drain and rinse the beans and put them in a
large saucepan with the bacon, vegetables, garlic,
bay leaf and thyme. Season with pepper and
cover generously with water. Bring to the boil
and boil rapidly for 10 minutes, then reduce the
heat, skim any scum from the surface, cover and
simmer for 1 hour.

Uncover the pan and continue to simmer for
a further hour, stirring occasionally. By this
time, the cooking liquid should have thickened
to a sauce. If the mixture is still very watery,
raise the heat and boil rapidly for a few minutes
to reduce. Stir in the butter and 2 tablespoons of
the parsley, and simmer for a further 15 minutes.
Taste and adjust the seasoning, adding salt if
required.

Meanwhile, cook the rice in plenty of boiling
salted water, until tender. White rice will need
15–20 minutes; brown rice will need 30–40
minutes. Drain well and pile in the centre of a
warmed deep dish. Spoon the beans around the
rice, sprinkle with the remaining 1 tablespoon
parsley and serve.

*Red Beans and Rice
Dry Spiced Butter Beans and Cauliflower*

MACARONI CHEESE

Preparation time: 10 minutes + 20–30 minutes cooking   Serves 4

250 g (8 oz) macaroni

2 tablespoons breadcrumbs

25 g (1 oz) mature Cheddar cheese, grated

salt

For the sauce:

25 g (1 oz) butter or 2 tablespoons olive oil

25 g (1 oz) plain flour

450 ml (¾ pint) milk

150 g (5 oz) mature Cheddar cheese, grated

1 teaspoon Dijon mustard, or 1 teaspoon Worcestershire sauce, or ¼ teaspoon Tabasco sauce

salt and pepper

Another classic pasta dish, macaroni cheese is no more than cooked pasta swathed in a good cheese sauce, then baked until brown and bubbling.

Preheat the oven to Gas Mark 6/200°C/400°F. Bring a large saucepan of lightly salted water to the boil and add the macaroni. Follow the packet instructions and cook for 8–10 minutes or until just *al dente* (tender but with a slight bite to it). Drain thoroughly.

Meanwhile, to make the sauce, heat the butter or oil in a saucepan, stir in the flour and continue stirring over a low heat for 1 minute. Remove from the heat and gradually add the milk, a little at a time, mixing it in well. Return the pan to the heat, bring the sauce slowly to the boil, stirring constantly, and simmer gently for 5 minutes, stirring frequently. Remove from the heat and stir in the cheese with the mustard, Worcestershire sauce or Tabasco sauce. Season with salt and pepper, and mix with the drained macaroni. Pour into a shallow buttered or oiled ovenproof dish.

Mix the breadcrumbs with the remaining cheese and sprinkle as evenly as possible over the surface. Bake in the oven for 20-30 minutes or until browned.

Note: If everything is still really hot when assembled, you can just put this under the grill for 5 minutes to brown the top.

FARFALLE WITH TUNA AND PEAS

Preparation and cooking time: 15–20 minutes   Serves 2

250 g (8 oz) farfalle or other pasta shapes

3 tablespoons olive or sunflower oil

1 small onion, sliced

1 garlic clove, chopped

¼ teaspoon hot chilli powder

99 g (3½ oz) can of tuna in oil, drained and flaked

50 g (2 oz) frozen peas, thawed

finely grated zest of ½ lemon

1 tablespoon lemon juice

1 tablespoon chopped fresh parsley

salt

Canned tuna, peas and lemon come together here to make a quick pasta sauce. Pasta shapes, such as farfalle or fusilli, are best for a 'bitty' sauce like this one.

Bring a large saucepan of lightly salted water to the boil and add the farfalle. Follow packet instructions and cook for 10–12 minutes or until the pasta is *al dente* (tender but with a slight bite to it).

As soon as the pasta is in the water, heat 2 tablespoons of the oil in a frying-pan and add the onion. Fry over a fairly high heat until beginning to brown. Add the garlic and chilli powder and cook for 1 minute longer. Reduce the heat and add the tuna, peas, lemon zest, lemon juice and a little salt. Cook for about 1 minute, stirring, then add the parsley.

Drain the pasta, toss it quickly with the remaining oil and turn it into a warmed bowl. Spoon the tuna sauce over it and serve immediately.

FISH

One of the best things about fish is that you don't have to do an awful lot to it. You can buy it ready-prepared, or you can choose a whole fish and ask at the fish counter for all the fiddly work, like cleaning, scaling and filleting, to be done for you, if necessary. Then when you get the fish home, it only takes a few minutes to cook. Neat.

The fresher fish is, the better it tastes. When choosing fresh fish, the first thing to check is the smell. Fresh fish smells of nothing more than the open sea; if it smells 'fishy', then it is stale. The eyes should be clear and bright, not misted over and shrunken. The gills should have a good red or pink colour and the skin should have a healthy sheen to it; avoid fish with dry, tired-looking skin. Finally, the flesh should be firm and plump.

Of course, many of these signs are not visible when it comes to selecting prepared fillets. In this case, check the smell, and choose fillets that look firm, fresh and pearly.

Once you've bought your fish, get it home and into the fridge as quickly as possible, then use it within 24 hours. Fish can be cooked in all sorts of ways and many of the best are also the simplest. For grilling, buy fish steaks or small whole fish, such as mackerel or trout. For frying, steaks, fillets or small whole fish are all suitable. Steaks and fillets can also be steamed or poached, and practically any cut or type of fish can be baked in the oven, wrapped in foil. Be careful not to overcook fish: when done, the flesh just flakes when tested with a knife point.

Fish with Citrus Fruit en Papillote
Baked Mackerel with Lemon and Rosemary

BAKED MACKEREL WITH LEMON AND ROSEMARY

Preparation time: 10 minutes + 20 minutes cooking   Serves 1

1 small to medium-sized
mackerel, cleaned

1 tablespoon lemon juice

1 teaspoon roughly chopped
fresh rosemary leaves, or ½
teaspoon dried rosemary

1 tablespoon olive or
sunflower oil

1½ teaspoons capers,
drained

salt and pepper

All the things that can be said in favour of herring go for mackerel as well; it is filling, tasty, cheap and healthy. In this recipe, lemon, capers and rosemary set off the richness of the fish to create a dish that is packed with flavour. However, if you don't have or don't like capers, the dish will still taste pretty good without them. For four people, use four mackerel, trimming off tails and heads if necessary to fit them in the dish. You'll only need 3 tablespoons each of lemon juice and oil, but multiply other quantities by four. The fish will probably take a little longer to cook — check after 25 minutes, but they may take as long as 30 minutes.

Preheat the oven to Gas Mark 4/180°C/350°F. Rinse the mackerel inside and out with cold water and pat dry with kitchen paper. Season the inside of the cavity with salt and pepper, a little of the lemon juice and a pinch of the rosemary.

Brush the inside of a shallow ovenproof dish with a little of the oil. Lay the mackerel in the dish and scatter with the capers and remaining rosemary. Season with salt and pepper and spoon over the remaining lemon juice and oil. Bake in the oven uncovered, for 20 minutes or until the fish is just cooked through to the bone. Baste once with its own juices half-way through the cooking time. Serve hot or cold.

FISH WITH CITRUS FRUIT EN PAPILLOTE

Preparation time: 20 minutes + 12 minutes cooking   Serves 4

4 large fillets of whiting, lemon sole or plaice

1 large orange

1 large lemon

2 tablespoons olive or sunflower oil

1 tablespoon chopped fresh parsley

1 tablespoon chopped fresh chives

salt and pepper

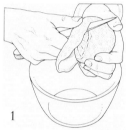

Baking en papillote, i.e. in a foil or paper parcel, is a simple and appealing way to cook fish. None of the flavour is lost; the fish is steamed to tenderness in its tight little capsule, absorbing the aromas of whatever else is in there with it. What's even more appealing is that there's no pan to wash up afterwards! If you want to make this just for yourself, season one fish fillet, lay it on oiled foil and add a squeeze of lemon juice, 1 teaspoon oil and some chopped fresh herbs. Cook as below.

Preheat the oven to Gas Mark 4/180°C/350°F. Season the fish fillets with salt and pepper. Grate about half the zest from the orange and lemon. Using a sharp knife and holding the fruit over a bowl to catch any juice, cut the peel and pith off the orange and lemon, right down to the flesh (Fig. 1). To cut out the segments of fruit, slice from top to bottom on each side of the pieces of white skin separating the segments (Fig. 2). Ease out the fruit nicely skinned and ready to use (Fig. 3).

Cut four large sheets of foil, each one large enough to enclose a fish fillet. Brush each sheet with oil. Set aside four segments of each of orange and lemon and divide the remaining segments between the pieces of foil. Lay the fillets, skin-side down, on top of the fruit, and scatter with parsley, chives and zest. Arrange the reserved orange and lemon segments on top, pour over any reserved fruit juice, and drizzle over the remaining oil.

Fold up the pieces of foil over the fish into loose parcels, sealing well and tucking the edges underneath. Place on a baking sheet and bake in the oven for 12 minutes. Serve immediately, giving each person their own parcel to unwrap.

GRILLED OR FRIED HERRING IN OATS

Preparation and cooking time: 15–20 minutes
plus chilling (optional)

Serves 1

*1 herring, cleaned and
scaled*

*1 teaspoon Dijon mustard
(optional)*

1 tablespoon plain flour

1 egg, lightly beaten

*about 3 tablespoons porridge
oats*

oil for frying

salt and pepper

a wedge of lemon, to serve

*Herring is a fish that we neglect rather foolishly. It has
the most delicious, rich flesh, is sold at a bargain price,
and is also incredibly good for you on top of all the
rest. The traditional Scottish way to cook it is rolled in
oats – the oats cook to a crisp, making a nice contrast
to the soft fish. If you are making this for more than
one person, you will find that one egg is enough to
coat two or three fish.*

Rinse the herring inside and out with cold
water, then pat dry with kitchen paper. Smear
the herring evenly with the mustard, if using.
Season the flour with salt and pepper and spread
on a plate. Put the beaten egg in a shallow dish,
and the oats on a second plate. Turn the herring
in the flour until lightly coated, shaking off the
excess, then dip into the egg. Shake off the
excess, and roll in the oats until well covered,
patting them down to coat evenly. At this point
you can put the herring in the fridge for 15
minutes (or until you need it), but bring it back
to room temperature before cooking.

Fry the herring in about 1 tablespoon oil over
a moderate heat until the oatmeal is brown and
the herring is just cooked through, turning once.
Alternatively, drizzle about ½ teaspoon oil over
each side of the herring, then cook under a
preheated medium grill, turning once, for about
8 minutes or until the oatmeal is brown and the
herring is just cooked through. Serve with the
lemon wedge to squeeze over.

GRILLED COLEY WITH CHEESE AND MUSTARD

Preparation and cooking time: 15–20 minutes · Serves 1

175 g (6 oz) coley fillet

25 g (1 oz) Gruyère or Cheddar cheese, grated finely

½ teaspoon Dijon mustard

2 teaspoons milk

a little oil for brushing

salt and pepper

Smothering fish with cheese and mustard may sound a little over the top, but surprisingly it's an excellent combination, and a quick one too. It goes particularly well with coley, which on its own can be rather a dull number.

Preheat the grill and line the grill rack with foil.

Season the fish lightly on both sides with salt and pepper. Mash the cheese firmly with the mustard and enough milk to make a very thick paste. Brush both sides of the fish lightly with oil, then grill, skin-side up (if it has any skin), about 5 cm (2 inches) away from the heat, on one side only, until lightly browned. Turn the fish over and grill the other side for 1–2 minutes or until the fish is almost cooked through. Spread the cheese paste thickly over the fish and return to the grill until the cheese is bubbling and browned. Serve immediately.

TROUT PLAKI

Preparation time: making the tomato sauce + 5 minutes
+ 25–30 minutes cooking

Serves 2

2 trout, scaled and cleaned

*1 quantity Chunky
Tomato Sauce (page 19)
made with 4 garlic cloves*

*2 tablespoons chopped fresh
parsley*

1 tablespoon olive oil

salt and pepper

Psaria plaki *is a Greek dish of fish baked in a
garlicky tomato sauce. I've used trout here, but you
can use whatever type of fish you like best, whether it
is whole fish, steaks or fillets (though fillets will cook
more quickly). If cooking for more than two people,
make enough sauce to cover all the fish, and remember
to allow a little longer cooking time.*

Preheat the oven to Gas Mark 4/180°C/350°F.
Rinse the trout inside and out with cold water,
then dry with kitchen paper. Season the inside
of the fish with salt and pepper.

Arrange the fish in a lightly oiled ovenproof
dish in which they fit together closely, curling
them round a little if necessary. Mix the tomato
sauce with the parsley and spoon over the fish.
Drizzle over the olive oil and bake in the oven
for 25–30 minutes or until the fish is just cooked
through.

CHICKEN AND MEAT

If I was told that I could only eat one type of meat for the rest of my life, it would have to be chicken: it is far and away the most versatile of meats. However, there are a few guidelines to remember when preparing and cooking poultry, since undercooked chicken may carry salmonella bacteria, which can cause food poisoning. Salmonella is destroyed by thorough cooking, so take these precautions:

• Keep raw chicken well wrapped in the fridge on the lowest shelf, where it can't drip on to food that will be eaten without further cooking.

• Wash your hands and all utensils thoroughly after preparing chicken.

• Make sure frozen chicken is *completely* thawed before cooking.

• To test if chicken is cooked right through, push a skewer or the tip of a small sharp knife right down into the thickest part of the joint or bird. Look at the juice that oozes out and have a quick peer at the flesh. If the juices run clear the chicken is cooked; if they run pink a few minutes' further cooking is required.

Red meats (beef, pork and lamb) provide important nutrients and, although pound for pound meat is more expensive than, say, carrots or cabbage, there are a fair number of cuts that won't make too big a dent in your budget.

Individual lamb or pork chops are great when you want a quick supper just for yourself, and minced beef is another good buy, but pick wisely: some mince contains a high percentage of fat. Streaky pork rashers and sausages are bargains, but again, they are relatively fatty so eat them only in moderation. If you have the time to make a proper beef stew (there's no quick way), then you can take advantage of less costly cuts, such as shin or chuck. Most stews taste even better when reheated, so make them in large quantities and reheat thoroughly, allowing them to bubble for at least 5 minutes, and adding a little extra water if needed.

GRILLED SPICED CHICKEN WITH YOGURT SAUCE

Preparation time: 5 minutes + marinating
+ 25–30 minutes cooking   Serves 2

*2 chicken quarters, thawed
if frozen*

salt

For the marinade:

¼ teaspoon ground cumin

*¼ teaspoon ground
coriander*

*¼ teaspoon freshly ground
black pepper*

*juice of ½ lime or ½ small
lemon*

*2 tablespoons olive or
sunflower oil*

For the sauce:

1 garlic clove, crushed

*1 tomato, skinned, de-
seeded and chopped finely*

*2 spring onions, chopped
finely*

*6 tablespoons greek-style
yogurt or natural fromage
frais*

salt and pepper

*This is a simple way to jazz up plain chicken with
aromatic spices and the sharpness of lime or lemon
juice. You can prepare the chicken up to a day in
advance.*

With a sharp knife, make three deep slashes
across the thickest parts of the chicken quarters
so that the heat of the grill can penetrate right
down into the meat. Place the chicken in a
shallow dish. Mix together the marinade
ingredients and pour over the chicken. Cover
and leave for at least 1 hour, and up to 24 hours,
turning occasionally. (If marinating for more
than 1 hour, store in the fridge, but bring back
to room temperature for 30 minutes before
grilling.) To make the sauce, mix all the
ingredients together. Taste and adjust the
seasoning, then cover and store in the fridge
until needed.

Preheat the grill. Remove the chicken from
the marinade, reserving the marinade, and grill
under a moderate heat for 25–30 minutes or
until just cooked through to the bone, turning
and brushing with marinade occasionally. If the
chicken seems to be browning too quickly on
the outside, adjust the grill rack so that it is a
little further away from the heat, or lower the
heat of the grill a little. Season with salt and
serve with the sauce.

*Grilled Spiced Chicken with Yogurt Sauce
Stir-fried Chicken with Broccoli and Red Pepper in Black
Bean Sauce*

STIR-FRIED CHICKEN WITH BROCCOLI AND RED PEPPER IN BLACK BEAN SAUCE

Preparation and cooking time: 20–25 minutes   Serves 2

2 boneless, skinless chicken breasts, thawed if frozen

175 g (6 oz) broccoli

1 red pepper, de-seeded

3 spring onions

1 tablespoon sunflower or vegetable oil

1 cm (½-inch) piece of fresh root ginger, peeled and chopped finely

1 garlic clove, chopped finely

½ fresh green chilli, de-seeded and chopped finely (optional)

For the sauce:

1½ tablespoons soy sauce

1½ tablespoons dry sherry or water

3 tablespoons black bean sauce

pepper

A shake of black bean sauce is a quick way to liven up a simple stir-fry. You'll find bottles of black bean sauce in the cooking sauce section of most supermarkets these days, and if you like the salty taste it's an excellent culinary investment, as good with plain vegetables as it is in this mixed dish of chicken, broccoli and red pepper. Stir-frying is an easy, quick and delicious method of cooking, but if you've never tried it before, make sure you read the notes in the Glossary of Basic Techniques in the introduction.

Cut the chicken into strips about 1 cm (½ inch) wide and 5 cm (2 inches) long. Break the broccoli florets into small pieces and slice the stems into discs about 5 mm (¼ inch) thick. Cut the red pepper into pieces about 1 cm (½ inch) wide and 2.5 cm (1 inch) long. Chop the spring onions into 2.5 cm (1 inch) lengths. Mix all the sauce ingredients in a small bowl.

Gather all the prepared ingredients together and put them on the work surface near the hob, so that they can be added to the pan without delay. Heat the oil in a wok or large frying-pan over a high heat. Keep the heat high throughout the cooking period. Drop the ginger, garlic and chilli, if using, into the hot oil and stir-fry for a few seconds. Add the broccoli and pepper, and stir-fry for about 2 minutes, keeping the vegetables constantly on the move.

Push the vegetables to one side of the wok or, if using a frying-pan, scoop them out and put them on a plate. Put the chicken and spring onions into the pan and stir-fry for 2–3 minutes or until the chicken is just cooked through. Mix the vegetables with the chicken. Quickly stir the sauce and pour it into the pan. Keep stirring and tossing for 2 more minutes, then serve immediately, with rice.

CORNED BEEF HASH

Preparation time: 20 minutes + standing (optional)
+ 30 minutes cooking

Serves 2–3

500 g (1 lb) potatoes, unpeeled

198 g (7 oz) can of corned beef, cubed

1 small onion, chopped finely

40 g (1½ oz) butter

1 tablespoon Worcestershire sauce

salt and pepper

1 tablespoon chopped fresh parsley, to garnish

This is a favourite Sunday brunch recipe. In a spare half hour on Saturday, I cook the potatoes and mix them with the corned beef and onions, then all there is to do on Sunday morning is to fry the whole lot up. It all comes together to make a wonderful, crisp and melting mass of meat and potatoes – a serious treat. It's not an elegant dish, but who cares when it tastes so good.

If you are serving the hash as a main course for supper, you might like to go right over the top and surmount each plateful with a poached or fried egg, serving a green or mixed salad on the side.

Cook the potatoes, leave to cool and then peel and dice them. Mix the corned beef, potatoes and onion, and season with a little salt and pepper. If you have time, leave for a few hours or overnight, covered, stirring occasionally, for the flavours to develop.

Melt the butter in a heavy-based frying pan and heat until foaming. Add the corned beef mixture and the Worcestershire sauce. Stir, then press down fairly firmly. Turn the heat down to medium-low and cook gently for about 15 minutes or until a brown crust forms on the base. Stir and break up, so that some of the crust gets mixed in with the remainder of the hash. Add about 5 tablespoons hot water, press down again and cook for a further 15 minutes or until a second crust has formed. Turn out on to a dish, scatter with parsley and serve immediately.

LAMB CHOP WITH MINT AND GARLIC

Preparation time: 5 minutes + 20 minutes cooking   Serves 1

½ garlic clove

2 leaves of fresh mint, or ¼ teaspoon dried mint

1 lamb chop

oil for brushing

pepper

Another quick way to jazz up a plain chop. It is simply spiked with mint (or you can use the leaves of a sprig of fresh rosemary instead) and slivers of garlic before grilling. This is excellent served with a simple sauce made from thick yogurt mixed with chopped fresh herbs, salt and pepper.

Preheat the grill to high. Cut the garlic into long thin slivers. If using fresh mint, cut it into strips. If using dried mint, toss the slivers of garlic in the mint to coat.

Using a small sharp knife, make little slits in the lamb and, using the tip of the knife to help, push slivers of garlic and strips of mint right down into the lamb, leaving just the tips showing. Brush the chop with oil and season with pepper only.

Grill the chop about 8 cm (3 inches) from the heat for 7–10 minutes or until nicely browned on each side. Serve immediately.

Bobotie

Lamb Chop with
Mint and Garlic

Corned Beef Hash

BOBOTIE

Preparation time: 15 minutes + 45–50 minutes cooking　　　Serves 4

15 g (½ oz) butter or 1 tablespoon oil

1 onion, chopped

1 garlic clove, chopped

1 thick slice of bread (about 50 g/2 oz)

150 ml (¼ pint) milk

500 g (1 lb) minced beef or lamb

1 tablespoon mild curry powder

½ tablespoon sugar

2 tablespoons lemon juice

25 g (1 oz) flaked almonds

75 g (3 oz) raisins

2 eggs

salt and pepper

Bobotie is a South African dish, and one of the best and easiest ways I know of transforming plain minced meat into something unusual and delicious. The mince is flavoured lightly with curry powder, almonds and raisins, and then topped with a savoury egg custard. It may sound a little bizarre, but it works! To make a larger quantity, double or treble the ingredients and bake in a roasting tin or large, shallow ovenproof dish. The mixture in the dish should be no more than 5 cm (2 inches) deep; if it is any deeper it may need a longer cooking time.

Preheat the oven to Gas Mark 4/180°C/350°F. Heat the butter or oil in a large frying-pan, add the onion and garlic and fry until lightly browned. Meanwhile, remove the crusts from the bread slice and soak the bread in the milk for 2–3 minutes. Squeeze the milk out of the bread, and reserve the bread and milk separately.

Mix the fried onion and garlic with the minced beef or lamb, curry powder, sugar, lemon juice, almonds, raisins and soaked bread. Season with salt and pepper and beat to mix evenly. Finally, beat in one of the eggs. Spoon the mixture into a greased 2-litre (3½-pint) dish and smooth down.

Beat the second egg with the reserved milk, season with salt and pepper, and pour over the minced meat mixture. Bake in the oven for 45–50 minutes or until the top is just set and browned.

GAMMON GLAZED PORK CHOPS

Preparation time: 5 minutes + 30–40 minutes cooking   Serves 2

2 pork chops, about 2 cm
(¾ inch) thick

1 teaspoon Dijon mustard

1½ tablespoons demerara or
muscovado sugar

juice of 1 small orange

This kind of glaze is often used for whole gammon joints, hence the name.

Preheat the oven to Gas Mark 3/160°C/325°F. Trim any excess fat from the chops and smear them with mustard on both sides. Sprinkle the sugar evenly over both sides of the chops, pressing it in gently to coat. Put the chops in a small, greased, ovenproof dish and pour over the orange juice. Bake in the oven for 30–40 minutes or until chops are cooked right through, basting occasionally with the pan juices.

ROAST CHICKEN WITH CELERY AND ORANGE STUFFING

Preparation time: 15 minutes + 1½ hours cooking   Serves 4

1.5–1.75 kg (3½–4 lb)
chicken, without giblets,
thawed if frozen

15 g (½ oz) butter

salt and pepper

For the stuffing:

25 g (1 oz) butter

1 onion, chopped

2 celery sticks, chopped

65 g (2½ oz) fresh white or
brown breadcrumbs

1 tablespoon chopped fresh
parsley

finely grated zest and juice
of 1 orange

1 egg, beaten

salt and pepper

A glistening, golden-brown roast chicken makes a wonderful meal, suitable for a special occasion or Sunday lunch shared with friends. Check very carefully that the chicken is cooked right through before you serve it; if you are in any doubt, return it to the oven for another 10–15 minutes.

Preheat the oven to Gas Mark 6/200°C/400°F. To make the stuffing, melt the butter in a small saucepan and heat until foaming. Add the onion and celery and cook gently until tender, without browning. Remove from the heat and add the breadcrumbs and parsley. Season with salt and pepper, and add the orange zest and juice. Mix well, then add just enough egg to make the mixture hold together, without making it sloppy.

Fill the chicken two-thirds full with the stuffing through the neck opening; do not pack too tightly. Tuck the flaps of skin in to enclose the stuffing. Weigh the stuffed chicken and calculate the cooking time, allowing 20 minutes per 500 g (1 lb), plus 20 minutes extra (i.e. if the

For the gravy:

1 tablespoon plain flour

300 ml (H pint) chicken stock, or vegetable cooking water

chicken weighs about 1.75 kg (4 lb) with the stuffing, then it will need 100 minutes – 4 × 20 minutes plus 20 minutes – in the oven). Smear the skin of the chicken with the 15 g (½ oz) butter and season with pepper. Place in a roasting tin and roast in the oven for the calculated time or until the chicken is cooked, basting it every 15–20 minutes with the juices in the tin. If the juices threaten to burn, add 1–2 tablespoons water.

The chicken is done when the thighs can be wiggled loosely in their joints. Test further by inserting a skewer into the flesh between the thigh and the breast – if the juices that run out are clear, then the chicken is cooked, but if they are pink it needs more time in the oven.

Lift the chicken on to a warmed serving dish and place in the oven, heat turned off and door slightly ajar, while you make the gravy. Pour all but about 1 tablespoon of fat out of the roasting tin. Place over a moderate heat and stir in the flour. Stir for 30–60 seconds or until lightly coloured. Stir in the stock or vegetable water and continue stirring until it boils. Simmer for 3–4 minutes, stirring occasionally. Adjust the seasoning and strain into a sauceboat or jug. Serve with the chicken.

Roast Chicken with Celery and Orange Stuffing

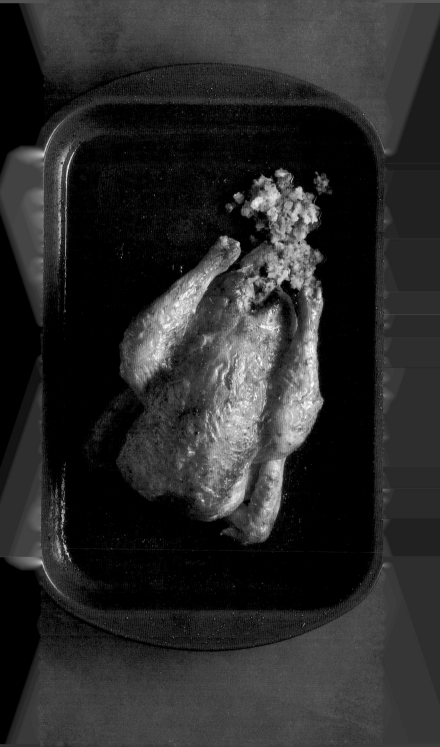

TEXAN CHILE CON CARNE

Preparation time: 45 minutes + about 3 hours cooking   Serves 4–6

1 kg (2 lb) brisket or braising beef

2 tablespoons plain flour

2 tablespoons oil

2 onions, sliced thinly

4 garlic cloves, chopped

250 g (8 oz) dried kidney beans, soaked overnight, or 2 × 432 g (14 oz) cans, drained and rinsed

½ teaspoon chilli powder

½ tablespoon ground cumin

1 heaped teaspoon dried oregano

900 ml–1.2 litres (1½–2 pints) water or chicken or beef stock

salt and pepper

A proper Texan-style chili (or chilli) con carne is made with chunks of beef, not mince, and is cooked long and slow to produce a magnificent dark stew. The seasoning can be made as hot as you like by increasing the quantity of chilli, but other spices add a subtler note.

Preheat the oven to gas Mark 6/200°C/400°F. Cut the beef into 2.5 cm (1-inch) cubes, trimming off any fat. Season the flour with salt and pepper. Toss the beef in the seasoned flour, shaking off any excess.

Heat the oil in a frying-pan over a moderate heat, and brown the beef fairly briskly in two or three batches. Transfer the meat to an ovenproof casserole dish. Fry the onion and garlic gently without browning in the same oil, adding a little extra if necessary. Place in the casserole, with the meat. Meanwhile, if using dried kidney beans, cover them with plenty of fresh water in a pan, bring to the boil, and boil vigorously for 10 minutes. Drain and add to the casserole, with a little pepper. Sprinkle over the chilli powder, cumin, and oregano.

Pour 900 ml (1½ pints) of the water or stock into the frying-pan, and bring up to the boil, scraping in the brown residues from frying. Pour into the casserole. Cover and place in the oven. After 20 minutes reduce heat to Gas Mark 2/150°C/300°F. Leave for a further 2–2½ hours, stirring occasionally. Add the canned kidney beans, if using, 30 minutes before the stew is done, and add more stock or water if it seems to be drying out. The stew is cooked when the meat is tender and the kidney beans are soft. Add salt to taste at this point.

TOAD IN THE HOLE

Preparation time: 35 minutes + 30 minutes standing   Serves 4
+ 35–40 minutes cooking

2 tablespoons oil, or 25 g
(1 oz) lard

500 g (1 lb) pork sausages,
pricked

For the batter:

125 g (4 oz) plain flour,
sifted

a pinch of salt

1 large egg (size 1–2)

300 ml (½ pint) milk

Basically, toad in the hole is sausages baked in
Yorkshire pudding – the poor man's replacement for a
big joint of roast beef with Yorkshire pudding. If you
use good meaty pork sausages, then it makes a first
class alternative.

To make the batter, mix the flour and salt in a
bowl. Make a hollow in the centre of the flour
and break the egg into it. Add a little of the
milk. Beat the eggs together with a spoon or
whisk, gradually drawing in the flour, and
adding more milk as the mixture thickens.
Continue beating until all the milk has been
added and you have a smooth batter. Set aside
for 30 minutes before using.
   Preheat the oven to Gas Mark 7/220°C/
425°F. Heat the oil or lard in a roasting tin, add
the sausages and fry over a high heat until
browned. Remove the sausages from the tin.
Tip and tilt the tin to coat the bottom with fat
and heat it through thoroughly. Quickly beat
the batter one more time, then pour it
immediately into the hot roasting tin. Add the
sausages, then bake in the oven for 35–40
minutes or until the batter is puffed and brown.
Serve immediately.

CARBONADES À LA FLAMANDE
(BEEF AND BEER CASSEROLE)

Preparation time: 20 minutes + 3 hours cooking   Serves 4–6

1 kg (2 lb) stewing beef

3–4 tablespoons plain flour

3–4 tablespoons oil

2 onions, sliced

2 garlic cloves, chopped

The liquid used in Carbonades à la Flamande is
brown ale, which gives a rich flavour to the sauce.
Otherwise, the basic method is exactly the same as for
all beef stews. Traditionally, no vegetables (other than
onions) are added to this stew, but if you want to
stretch it a little further, you can add a few sliced
carrots or celery sticks to the pan with the meat.

300 ml (½ pint) brown ale, lager or stout

1 tablespoon light muscovado sugar

bouquet garni (1 bay leaf, a sprig of parsley and a sprig of thyme tied together with string)

about 300 ml (½ pint) water

salt and pepper

For the crust:

25 g (1 oz) butter, softened

1 tablespoon Dijon mustard

6 slices of French bread

This is an excellent dish to cook for a large group of people, but you will need a very big casserole, and so much beef can be expensive. If you double, or even treble, the quantities, cook the onions in two batches and the beef in four or five batches. Add enough water to cover the meat in the casserole and allow an extra 30 minutes cooking in the oven.

Preheat the oven to Gas Mark 3/150°C/325°F. Cut the beef into strips about 1 cm (½-inch) thick, 8 cm (3 inches) long and 2.5 cm (1 inch) wide. Season the flour with a little salt and pepper, then toss the beef in the flour until it is evenly coated.

Heat 2 tablespoons of the oil in a large frying-pan, add the onions and fry over a moderate heat until tender. Add the garlic and continue cooking for 2 minutes, then scoop the onion and garlic out of the pan and put them in the bottom of an ovenproof casserole. Raise the heat under the frying-pan, add half the meat and fry briskly until browned on all sides. Remove from the pan and put in the casserole. Brown the remaining beef in the same way, adding a little extra oil to the pan if necessary. Put the second batch of beef in the casserole.

Turn down the heat under the frying-pan, and pour in the beer. Bring to the boil, stirring and scraping in all the browned bits left in the pan. Stir in the sugar, then pour over the meat and onions. Add the bouquet garni and season with salt and pepper. Add enough of the water to cover the beef. Cover the casserole and cook in the oven for 2½ hours, stirring occasionally and adding a little more water if it gets too dry. (The casserole can be cooked up to this point a day in advance, then reheated in the oven before adding the crust.)

Mash the butter with the mustard and spread it thickly on the bread slices. Uncover the casserole and place the bread, buttered side up on the stew. Return the stew to the oven and cook, uncovered, for 30 minutes or until the bread is crisp and lightly browned on top. Serve straight away.

Carbonades à la Flamande (Beef and Beer Casserole)

VEGETABLES AND SALADS

People who say they don't like vegetables worry me. When there are so many different types to choose from, with so many different tastes and textures and so many possible ways of cooking them, how can they possibly know that they dislike all of them? As well as being endlessly versatile and delicious, vegetables are cheap, and they are of major importance to health (they are full of fibre and vitamins), so eat as many as you can, raw and cooked, every day.

The main principle to remember when cooking vegetables is never to overdo it. Mushy, overcooked vegetables lose so much of their flavour, and in some cases become rather unpleasant, so err on the side of undercooking rather than overcooking. If you are steaming, boiling or microwaving vegetables, stop the cooking when they are more or less *al dente*, that is just tender but still with a slight bite to them at the very centre.

Most of the recipes in this chapter are for slightly more involved methods of cooking particular vegetables. Quite a few of them are substantial enough to stand as a main course on their own, while others are better served as side dishes or perhaps for a first course.

FRENCH DRESSING (VINAIGRETTE)

Preparation time: 5 minutes   Serves 4-6

1 tablespoon wine vinegar or cider vinegar

½ teaspoon Dijon mustard (optional)

a pinch of sugar (optional)

4 tablespoons sunflower, groundnut or olive oil

salt and pepper

There's nothing simpler than making a vinaigrette, but it does rely on a good balance of ingredients. It's important to taste the vinaigrette once made; some vinegars are more acidic than others, so you may need to add a little more oil. When the dressing is made, you should be able to taste the vinegar in it, but it shouldn't be strong enough to pucker up your mouth. Vinaigrette will keep for 4–5 weeks in a screw-top jar in the fridge.

Put all the ingredients in a screw-top jar, screw on the lid and shake vigorously. Taste and adjust the seasoning, adding more oil if the dressing is on the sharp side.

Alternatively, put the vinegar in a bowl and add the mustard and sugar, if using. Season with salt and pepper, and whisk in the oil a tablespoon at a time. Taste and adjust the seasoning, adding more oil if the dressing is on the sharp side. If you use this second method, you can make the dressing in the serving bowl, then put the salad ingredients in on top and toss together before serving.

Variation: For an Italian (or Greek) dressing, shake or whisk together 1½ tablespoons lemon juice and 4–5 tablespoons olive oil. Season with salt and pepper.

GREEN SALAD

There's no one single recipe for a green salad, largely because there is such a wide choice of ingredients. This is the basic method, with a few tips for making a good green salad.

First of all, choose a lettuce with some substance to it. Crisp or cos lettuces make good salads, while continental varieties, such as the slightly bitter frisée, or the green or bronze feuille de chêne, add interest. You can also buy bags of ready-prepared mixed salad leaves. Assuming, though, that you are starting with a whole lettuce, first separate and wash the leaves, tearing larger ones into two or three pieces to make them more manageable. Dry well, either in a salad spinner or wrapped in a clean tea towel. Lettuce will stay crisp for up to 2 days if stored in a polythene bag in the fridge.

Make a vinaigrette (page 67) and pour some into a salad bowl (or make it in the salad bowl). Don't use too much – ½ a tablespoon is plenty for a one-person salad, and 3–4 tablespoons is enough for four. There should be just enough

Ratatouille

dressing to coat the leaves lightly, without drenching them. Add the lettuce just before serving, and toss only when you are about to eat the salad, so that the leaves don't start to wilt in the dressing.

Variations: If you like garlic, add a crushed garlic clove to the dressing. A handful of roughly chopped fresh herbs can be tossed in with the leaves. Small croûtons add crunch and contrast, as do a scattering of roughly broken-up walnuts, or pine kernels.

Green Salad, with French Dressing (Vinaigrette)

Tomato Salad, with mozzarella cheese

RATATOUILLE

Preparation time: 50 minutes + 50 minutes cooking   Serves 6–8

1 large aubergine, cut in 2.5 cm (1-inch) chunks

500 g (1 lb) courgettes, cut in 1 cm (½-inch) slices

4 tablespoons olive or sunflower oil

1 large onion, chopped

2 garlic cloves, chopped

1 red and 1 green pepper, de-seeded and cut in 1 cm (½-inch) slices

397 g (14 oz) can of chopped tomatoes

1 tablespoon tomato purée

½ teaspoon sugar

½ teaspoon coriander seeds

salt and pepper

2 tablespoons chopped fresh basil or parsley, to serve

When made properly, ratatouille is one of the most outstanding vegetable dishes in the world. It's every bit as good cold as a first course, or hot as a side dish, or even as a main course if you poach an egg or two in it as it simmers on top of the stove. Never try to rush the cooking of ratatouille – the secret of success lies in long, gentle simmering. If you want to make double or even treble quantities, make sure you have a big enough pan, and allow plenty of extra cooking time – judge when it's done by look and taste.

Put the aubergine and courgettes into a colander and sprinkle with ½ tablespoon salt. Leave for 30 minutes to drain, then rinse and pat dry with kitchen paper.

Heat the oil in a large frying-pan or saucepan, add the onion and garlic, and fry gently until tender but not brown. Add the aubergine and peppers, stir, then cover and cook for 10 minutes, over a low heat stirring once or twice. Add the courgettes, tomatoes, tomato purée and sugar. Season with salt and pepper and bring to the boil, then lower the heat and simmer gently, uncovered, for about 30 minutes, stirring occasionally to prevent burning.

Crush the coriander seeds in a pestle and mortar or in a strong bowl with the end of a rolling pin or bottle. Stir the coriander into the pan and continue cooking for about another 10 minutes, stirring frequently, until all traces of wateriness have gone and the ratatouille is thick and rich. Taste and adjust the seasoning, adding a little more sugar if the flavour is on the sharp side. Serve hot or cold, sprinkled with basil or parsley.

TOMATO SALAD

For a good tomato salad, you need to start with good tomatoes, in other words tomatoes that are sweet, juicy and full of flavour. Italian plum tomatoes are usually a good choice, but experiment with different varieties to find one you like that has a good flavour. As well as the variations given below, you could also add some black olives, capers or strips of anchovy.

Allow one medium-size tomato per person. Slice the tomatoes and arrange the slices on a plate. Drizzle over a generous teaspoon of vinaigrette (page 67) per tomato, and then scatter with roughly torn fresh basil leaves, or chopped fresh chives, parsley, marjoram or oregano.

Variations: Add thinly sliced rings of onion (preferably red). One slice of onion is enough per tomato. Alternatively, for every two tomatoes in a plain tomato salad, add one orange, peeled and thinly sliced.

For a tomato and mozzarella salad for four people, slice one 150 g (5 oz) ball of mozzarella and four tomatoes. Arrange on a plate, drizzle over 2–3 tablespoons vinaigrette (page 67), sprinkle with freshly ground black pepper and scatter with torn-up basil leaves.

STIR-FRIED VEGETABLES

Preparation and cooking time: 15 minutes   Serves 2

2 leeks

1 tablespoon sunflower or
vegetable oil

1 cm (½ inch) piece of fresh
root ginger, peeled and
chopped finely

1 garlic clove, chopped finely

125 g (4 oz) button
mushrooms, quartered

50 g (2 oz) bean sprouts

1 tablespoon soy sauce

1 teaspoon sesame oil
(optional)

pepper

Think of this more as a method than as a definitive recipe. It can be adapted to fit most quick-cooking vegetables. The important thing is to add the vegetables to the pan in the right order. Start with those that require the longest cooking time (e.g. carrots, cauliflower or broccoli) and work up to those that require the least cooking (e.g. bean sprouts or mangetout). Don't overcrowd the pan, or the vegetables won't cook properly.

This simple recipe uses just garlic, ginger, soy sauce and sesame oil (optional) for flavouring. If you want to be a little more adventurous, try finishing with black bean, hoisin or oyster sauce, all of which can be bought in bottles.

Trim the root ends and tough green tops from the leeks and cut the remaining white parts diagonally into 5 mm (¼ inch) slices. Rinse thoroughly under running cold water, then drain well and dry.

Heat the oil in a wok or large frying-pan over a high heat. Keep the heat high throughout cooking. Add the ginger and garlic, stir, then add the leeks and stir-fry for 1 minute. Add the mushrooms and continue stir-frying for 2–3 minutes or until the mushrooms are beginning to soften, the leeks are lightly patched with brown, and any liquid given off by the mushrooms has sizzled away. Throw in the bean sprouts and continue stir-frying for a further 1 minute. Finally, pour over the soy sauce and sesame oil, if using, and season with pepper. Stir to mix and as soon as the liquid has all been absorbed, remove from the heat and serve.

Pictured also on the back cover.

Stir-fried Vegetables

BAKED POTATOES

Preparation time: 5 minutes + 45 minutes–1½ hours cooking

1 medium–large potato per person

oil

salt

To serve:

butter and grated cheese, or soured cream or yogurt mixed with chopped fresh chives.

Baked potatoes are tremendous all-rounders – the great fall-back when times are lean or the urge to cook is at its lowest ebb – and they can form the basis for a simple main course, or an accompaniment to anything from a plate of ham and salad to a spicy chilli con carne. They are not quick to cook, to be sure, but they are almost effortless. When you're baking a potato for yourself, make the most of the oven heat by slipping in an extra one or two to be used for mashed potatoes the next day.

Choose a 'floury' textured potato for baking, such as Kerr's Pink, Cara or King Edward. Sweet potatoes can also be baked this way. If you are already cooking something in the oven at anywhere between Gas Mark 4–7/180–220°oC/350–424°F, you can bake potatoes at the same time, though you will need to allow a little more or less time.

Preheat the oven to Gas Mark 6/200°C/400°F. Scrub the potato(es) well and prick with a fork. Rub or brush with oil, and rub salt into the skin. Bake in the oven for 45 minutes–1 hour or until tender. (You can speed up the cooking time by pushing a metal skewer through the centre.)

To serve, split the potato(es) open and add a generous knob of butter and some grated cheese, or soured cream or yogurt mixed with chopped chives.

EGG-STUFFED BAKED POTATO

Preparation time: 5 minutes + 55 minutes–1¼ hours cooking   Serves 1

1 large potato

1 egg

a knob of butter

salt and pepper

Bake the potato as on page 74, but don't turn off the oven. Slice the top off the potato and scoop out a hollow in the potato large enough to hold the egg. Season with salt and pepper. Carefully crack open the egg and slip it into the hollow. Season with pepper only (salt hardens the yolk), top with a knob of butter and then replace the potato lid. Return to the oven for 7–10 minutes or until the egg is cooked.

HASSELBACK POTATOES

Preparation time: 10 minutes + 45–55 minutes cooking   Serves 4

8 × 125 g (4 oz) potatoes

4 tablespoons olive or sunflower oil

salt and pepper

The thing I like best about roast potatoes is the crispy skin. Well, with hasselback potatoes you get double rations. What could be better? They require a little extra preparation, but it's worth it. Use a moderately 'waxy' type of potato – either large new potatoes or small Cara. The cooking time depends on the size of the potatoes (125 g/4 oz each is a rough guide, not absolutely obligatory), so check one or two of them towards the end of the cooking time by slipping a skewer or knife point between the 'leaves', down into the thickest part of the base.

Preheat the oven to Gas Mark 7/220°C/425°F. Peel the potatoes, and cut a thin slice off one long side of each one so that they can stand firmly. Using a sharp knife, slice each potato downwards almost to the flat base but not quite, so that the slices hold together like the pages of a book. Each slice should be about 5 mm (¼ inch) thick.

    Sit the potatoes, cut-sides up, in an oiled ovenproof dish or small roasting tin. Drizzle over the oil and season with salt and pepper. Bake in the oven for 45–55 minutes, basting occasionally with the oil in the dish, until the potatoes are nicely browned on the outside, and cooked through on the inside.

CURRIED VEGETABLE PASTIES

Preparation time: 40 minutes + 30 minutes resting
+ 25–30 minutes cooking

Makes 4

1½ tablespoons sunflower or vegetable oil

½ onion, chopped

1 potato, cut into 1 cm (½-inch) cubes

1 large carrot, cut into 1 cm (½-inch) cubes

½ red or green pepper, de-seeded and cut into 1 cm (½-inch) cubes

50 g (2 oz) frozen peas, thawed

1–2 teaspoons curry paste

500 g (1 lb) shortcrust pastry, thawed if frozen

1 egg, beaten, or milk, to glaze

salt

These pasties are just the thing for a packed lunch or a light meal, served perhaps with a green and/or tomato salad. Once you've got the idea of how to make them, you can vary the vegetables included according to what you have available. There are many types of curry paste; I usually use Madras curry paste which is medium-hot, but you may prefer a milder blend, or a much hotter one.

Heat the oil in a frying-pan, add the onion, potato, carrot and pepper, and fry over a medium heat until they begin to brown, stirring frequently. Add the peas and 4 tablespoons of water, and stir in the curry paste. Reduce the heat, cover and cook for 5 minutes or until the vegetables are just tender. Cool slightly and add salt to taste.

Quarter the pastry, and roll each piece out on a lightly floured surface to give a circle about 15 cm (6 inches) in diameter. Divide the vegetable mixture between the four circles, brush the edges with egg, and fold the pastry over the filling to form semicircles, pressing the edges together firmly. If you have time, leave the pasties to rest for 30 minutes in the fridge.

Preheat the oven to Gas Mark 6/200°C/ 400°F. Put the pasties on a greased baking sheet and brush with egg. Bake in the oven for 25–30 minutes or until nicely browned. Eat hot or cold.

Hasselback Potatoes
Curried Vegetable Pasties

SWEET THINGS

On a day-to-day basis, the best way to round off a meal is with a piece of fruit, but for a special treat there's nothing better than a home-made pudding.

When you are deciding what pudding to make, the first thing to consider is timing. Many puddings can be made in advance, which makes life a great deal easier when it comes to serving up, but is hopeless if you don't have time to cook earlier in the day. A lot of quick puddings may need last-minute preparation, which is fine as long as there's enough space left between the dirty dishes, and you don't mind doing a little work between courses.

Choose a pudding to fit in with the rest of your menu. If the main part of the meal has been very filling, then opt for a light, fruit-based pudding. Conversely, if you are keen to make a fairly stodgy pudding, then keep the main part of the meal light and not too filling. Use your common sense and choose a pudding that balances out the rest of the meal, but that is still a delicious indulgent finale.

CHOCOLATE SAUCE

Preparation and cooking time: 15 minutes Serves 4–6

175 g (6 oz) caster sugar

300 ml (½ pint) water

75 g (3 oz) Deluxe Plain Cooking Chocolate, broken into squares

25 g (1 oz) cocoa powder

This is wonderful poured over vanilla ice cream. If you double the quantity you will need to simmer the sauce for an extra 2 minutes. Any leftovers can be kept in the fridge for a week (if you can resist!).

Put all the ingredients in a saucepan and stir over a low heat until the sugar and chocolate have completely dissolved. Raise the heat and bring to the boil, then reduce the heat again and simmer for 8 minutes, stirring occasionally. Serve hot or cold.

HOT BANANAS WITH APRICOT SAUCE

Preparation and cooking time: 10–12 minutes   Serves 4

4 bananas

single cream, greek-style yogurt or natural fromage frais, to serve

For the sauce:

250 g (8 oz) apricot jam

juice of 1 orange

This was one of my mother's recipes, and is one that I return to frequently. With the apricot sauce and cream it is special enough (and easy enough) to serve for a dinner party, and when I'm on my own, I occasionally treat myself to a single grilled banana, with just a dollop of fromage frais. The apricot sauce can be made up to 24 hours in advance and warmed through when needed.

To make the sauce, put the apricot jam and orange juice in a saucepan and stir over a moderate heat until evenly mixed and gently simmering. Sieve. That's it.

The bananas can be boiled or grilled, whichever is easiest. To boil, bring a large saucepan of water to the boil, drop the unpeeled bananas into it and boil for 4 minutes. Drain. To grill, preheat the grill, and grill the bananas for about 6 minutes, turning once or twice, until the skin is dark, and the bananas are sizzling. Reheat the sauce gently while the bananas are cooking.

To serve, put a whole hot banana on each plate and peel off a strip of skin to reveal the soft, scented, steaming flesh. The warm apricot sauce can then be spooned over, along with some cream, yogurt or fromage frais.

PEANUT BUTTER COOKIES

Preparation time: 25 minutes + 18–24 minutes cooking

Makes about 30

125 g (4 oz) butter, softened

200 g (7 oz) light muscovado sugar

200 g (7 oz) crunchy peanut butter

1 egg

½ teaspoon vanilla essence

150 g (5 oz) plain flour, sifted

½ teaspoon salt

½ teaspoon bicarbonate of soda

Even though I'm not that fond of peanut butter, I love these biscuits. They are sweet and crumbly and ooh, another one please. Use crunchy peanut butter, not the smooth sort, so that you get pleasing nuggets of peanut dotted through the biscuits.

Preheat the oven to Gas Mark 5/190°C/375°F. Cream the butter and sugar together until light and fluffy. Gradually beat in the peanut butter, then the egg and the vanilla essence. Sift the flour with the salt and bicarbonate of soda, then mix it into the peanut butter mixture.

Line two baking sheets with non-stick baking parchment, or grease with butter. Place dessertspoonfuls of the mixture on the sheets leaving a good 8 cm (3 inches) of space around each one. Press down flat with a lightly floured spoon or a palette knife and bake in the oven for 9–12 minutes or until firm. Continue baking in batches until all the mixture has been used. Cool the biscuits on a wire rack.

*Hot Bananas with
Apricot Sauce*

Eve's Pudding

Peanut Butter Cookies

EVE'S PUDDING

Preparation time: 20 minutes + 30–35 minutes cooking   Serves 4

750 g (1½ lb) cooking apples

75 g (3 oz) caster sugar

½ teaspoon ground cinnamon

For the sponge:

50 g (2 oz) butter, softened

50 g (2 oz) caster sugar

1 egg, lightly beaten

125 g (4 oz) self-raising flour

a pinch of salt

3 tablespoons milk

finely grated zest of 1 lemon

This is a truly heartwarming winter pudding – a layer of apple topped with a light sponge. It doesn't take very long to make and is best eaten straight from the oven, though it can be kept warm for a while. A larger pudding can be made simply by doubling or trebling the quantities as appropriate, but unless you have a food processor this means a lot of hard arm-work. You may need to cook a larger pudding for 5–10 minutes longer – judge 'doneness' by touch not time.

Preheat the oven to Gas Mark 6/200°C/400°F. Butter a pie dish. Peel, core and thinly slice the apples. Toss with the caster sugar and the cinnamon, and spread in the bottom of the pie dish.

Put the butter in a bowl and cream until very soft. Add the sugar and continue beating until the mixture is light and fluffy. Beat in the egg, a little at a time. Sift the flour with the salt and beat into the mixture in spoonfuls, alternating with splashes of the milk to give the mixture a dropping consistency, i.e. it drops slowly off the spoon if you hold a spoonful above the bowl. Fold in the lemon zest and spread the mixture over the apples.

Bake the pudding in the oven for 30–35 minutes or until the topping is firm to the touch. Serve immediately, or leave in the oven, heat off and door slightly ajar, for up to 20 minutes before eating.

BUTTERSCOTCH SAUCE

Preparation and cooking time: 10 minutes　　　　　　Serves 4–6

50 g (2 oz) unsalted butter

175 g (6 oz) light
muscovado sugar

2 tablespoons golden syrup

a pinch of salt

142 ml (¼ pint) carton of
double cream

This is delicious with vanilla ice cream. If you are
looking for an easy pudding to serve at a dinner party,
you could make up one quantity of this sauce and one
quantity of Chocolate Sauce (page 78) so your guests
have a choice of sauces to pour over their ice cream.
However, if you prefer to serve a double quantity of
this sauce, simply increase the ingredients accordingly.
Butterscotch sauce will keep happily in the fridge for a
week.

Put all the ingredients in a saucepan and stir over
a low heat until the sugar has completely
dissolved. Bring to the boil, stirring, then draw
off the heat.

Note: Golden syrup is much easier to spoon out
of the tin if you use a metal spoon that has been
heated by dipping in boiling water first.

JAM ICE CREAM

Preparation time: 7 minutes + 8–10 hours freezing　　　　　Serves 6

375 g (12 oz) good quality
jam

2 tablespoons lemon juice

300 ml (½ pint) carton of
whipping or double cream

This is probably the world's quickest ever ice cream. It
is important to choose a good quality jam with a high
fruit content, such as an 'extra' jam or conserve.
Apricot jam makes particularly fine ice cream, but
other flavours give good results too. Before you throw it
together, make sure there's enough space in the freezer
compartment of your fridge to take the finished ice
cream. Ice cream will keep happily in the freezer for a
couple weeks, so even if there aren't six of you to eat it
at one fell swoop it's worth making up the full
quantity and saving some for a later date. For larger
numbers, just double or treble the quantities, but
remember that it will take much more effort to whip
the cream, and you'll need extra space in the freezer.

Beat the jam with the lemon juice until smooth.
Whip the cream until it just holds its shape, then
fold the cream into the jam. Spoon into a

freezerproof container (plastic, china or glass) and freeze for 8–10 hours or overnight.

COCONUT FRUIT CRUMBLE

Preparation time: 30–35 minutes + 30–40 minutes cooking   Serves 6

75 g (3 oz) caster sugar

1 teaspoon ground cinnamon

225 ml (7½ fl oz) water

175 g (6 oz) ready-to-eat dried apricots, chopped roughly

625–750 g (1¼–1½ lb) cooking apples, peeled, cored and chopped roughly

3 bananas, peeled and sliced

For the crumble:

175 g (6 oz) plain flour

75 g (3 oz) butter, diced

75 g (3 oz) caster sugar

25 g (1 oz) desiccated coconut

This is an interesting variation on the traditional fruit crumble, with a topping flavoured with coconut, and a mixture of fruit hidden away underneath. You can, of course, use just apples on their own, in which case you'll need to increase their quantity to 1–1.1 kg (2–2½ lb). Prepare as below, then sprinkle with sugar and a little cinnamon before covering with crumble topping.

Preheat the oven to Gas Mark 6/200°C/400°F. Put the sugar, cinnamon and water in a saucepan and stir over a medium heat for about 5 minutes or until the sugar has completely dissolved. Bring to the boil and add the apricots. Simmer gently for 8–10 minutes or until the apricots are tender. Remove from the heat and leave to cool slightly. Spread the apples in an ovenproof dish. Scatter over the banana, then spoon over the apricots and their syrup.

To make the crumble, put the flour in a bowl. Rub in the butter until the mixture resembles breadcrumbs, then mix in the sugar and coconut. Sprinkle lightly and evenly over the fruit. Bake in the oven for 30–40 minutes or until the crumble is nicely browned.

Jam Ice Cream
Coconut Fruit Crumble

CHOCOLATE MOUSSE

Preparation time: 10–15 minutes + chilling   Serves 4

*125 g (4 oz) Deluxe Plain
Cooking Chocolate*

4 eggs, separated

*Everyone loves chocolate mousse, and it is one of the
easiest puddings to make. Very convenient. The key
to making a really good one is to choose the best
chocolate. Have a look at the wrapper; somewhere it
will tell you what percentage of cocoa solids it contains.
The higher the percentage, the better the chocolate. A
chocolate containing at least 50 per cent cocoa solids is
ideal for chocolate mousse. A whisk is necessary for
this recipe.*

*To make this mousse for more than four people,
add another 25 g (1 oz) chocolate and 1 egg for each
additional person. However, whisking more than four
egg whites by hand takes a lot of arm-power, so you
might need some help!*

Break the chocolate into squares and put it in a
heatproof bowl. Set the bowl over a saucepan of
gently simmering water, making sure that the
base of the bowl does not touch the water. Take
care not to overheat or the chocolate will
become grainy. Stir occasionally, until the
chocolate has melted and is runny – a matter of
a few minutes so don't wander off and leave it.
As soon as the chocolate has melted, lift the
bowl off the pan (wear ovengloves or use a tea
towel as the bowl will be hot).

One by one, beat the egg yolks into the
melted chocolate. Whisk the egg whites until
they form stiff peaks. Stir 1 tablespoon of the
egg white into the chocolate mixture until
evenly mixed, then carefully and lightly fold in
the remaining egg whites with a large metal
spoon, until no white flecks are visible. Pour the
mixture into one serving bowl or four individual
bowls and chill until set.

Variations: Add 1½ tablespoons orange juice,
brandy or orange liqueur to the chocolate
mixture after beating in the egg yolks.

PARTIES

Catering without fluster for larger numbers of people throws up special problems, but none that can't be solved with a bit of advance planning. For a start, do you have enough plates, cutlery, and glasses? If you can't borrow the extras, you'll have to buy paper plates and plastic cutlery, so add them to your shopping list. When you're planning what to cook, check that you have enough pans of the right size.

Next: the food. Above all don't be over-ambitious: remember that the main point of the event is to get together and enjoy each other's company. Many of the recipes in this book can be made in greater volume, and in this chapter, you'll find more ideas for generous feasting.

If you're planning a three-course meal, choose a first course and a pudding that can be prepared in advance, and just reheated if necessary. A bowl of soup or a selection of dips, served with crudités and warm pitta bread, or cold vegetable dishes, such as Tabbouleh (page 88), or Ratatouille page 70) served with hunks of good bread always goes down well. For pudding, the simplest thing is a bowl of fruit and some cheese and crackers, or choose a pudding from this book.

But what about the main course? I usually opt for a big one-pot or one-tray solution. Most stews actually taste better made a day in advance and reheated. Spicy Vegetable Couscous (page 92) is one of my constant standbys; it satisfies both vegetarians and meat-eaters.

Lastly, there are side-dishes to consider. As often as not, I stick with a big green or mixed salad. With a stew-type dish I'd add some rice or potatoes, but if pushed for time or space, you can get away with laying on plenty of decent bread to mop up the juices.

Finally, don't panic if something goes wrong. Nine times out of ten no one will notice. The main thing is to enjoy yourself: if you're having a good time, then the chances are that your guests are too!

TABBOULEH

Preparation time: 30 minutes

Serves 8

250 g (8 oz) bulgar wheat or couscous

250 g (8 oz) tomatoes, de-seeded and chopped very finely

½ cucumber, chopped very finely

5 spring onions, chopped finely

a bunch of fresh mint, chopped finely

a bunch of fresh parsley, chopped finely

4–6 tablespoons olive oil

2–3 tablespoons lemon juice

salt and pepper

This Middle Eastern salad is best made the day before it is to be served, which is handy when you're cooking for lots of friends. Bulgar wheat is cracked wheat; you could use couscous instead, which, like bulgar, only needs soaking before use. To adjust the quantities, halve or multiply the ingredients, as necessary, but rely on taste to determine the correct balance of oil, lemon juice and seasoning.

Put the bulgar wheat or couscous in a bowl and pour over enough boiling water to cover. Leave to soak for 15 minutes, then drain and squeeze out as much water as you can with your hands or in a clean tea towel. Mix the bulgar or couscous with the vegetables and stir in the herbs. Add 4 tablespoons olive oil and 2 tablespoons lemon juice, and season with salt and pepper. Mix well, then taste and adjust the seasoning, adding more oil and lemon juice if required. Cover and refrigerate for at least 4 hours, preferably 24 hours. Just before serving, stir and taste again to check the seasoning.

French Bread Pizzas

Tabbouleh

FRENCH BREAD PIZZAS

Preparation time: making Tomato Sauce + 6–10 minutes
+ 3–4 minutes cooking   Serves 6–16 (see below)

2 baguettes

olive oil

2 garlic cloves (optional)

For the toppings:

1 quantity very thick
Tomato Sauce, made with
chopped tomatoes (page 19)

2 × 150 g (5 oz) ball of
mozzarella cheese, diced

24 black olives, halved and
pitted (optional)

16 anchovy fillets, cut in
half lengthways (optional)

198 g (7 oz) can of tuna in
oil, drained and flaked
(optional)

1 red pepper, de-seeded and
cut into small, thin strips
(optional)

50 g (2 oz) peperoni
(optional)

½ tablespoon dried oregano
or marjoram

pepper

olive oil

*This is a recipe with a lot of leeway for improvisation.
I've made a few suggestions for things to top the
'pizzas' with, but they're not mandatory. Use your
imagination, and add whatever you like to eat on an
ordinary pizza, as long as it doesn't need more than
the briefest of cooking.*

*If you are serving this as a main course, then there
should be just enough to stretch around 6 people, as
long as you serve a generous salad or two with it, and
follow with a good pudding. If you want to serve it as
a first course of one piece per person, then it will go
around a full 16!*

*You can prepare everything well in advance, but
don't put it all together until the last moment.*

Cut each baguette into four pieces, then split
each piece in half lengthways. Brush the cut
sides lightly with oil, then grill until golden
brown and rub with the raw garlic cloves
(optional, but great if you love garlic). This can
be done several hours in advance.

Preheat the grill. Arrange the baguette pieces,
cut sides up, on baking sheets. Spread each one
with tomato sauce, then scatter with mozzarella.
Choose between the olives, anchovies, tuna, red
pepper and peperoni, arranging a combination
of two or more of these on each 'pizza'. Sprinkle
with oregano and pepper. Drizzle a little olive
oil over each one, then place under the grill
until the cheese has melted and is beginning to
brown. Serve immediately.

CHICKEN CASSOULET

Preparation time: 5–10 minutes + 1½–1¾ hours cooking   Serves 8

4 tablespoons olive or sunflower oil

8 chicken thighs

175 g (6 oz) streaky bacon, de-rinded and cut into strips

1 large onion, chopped

2 carrots, chopped

6 garlic cloves, crushed

500 g (1 lb) passata or creamed tomatoes

1 tablespoon tomato purée

1 teaspoon sugar

1 bay leaf

2 sprigs of fresh thyme, or 1 teaspoon dried thyme

1 sprig of fresh rosemary, or ½ teaspoon dried rosemary

4 tablespoons chopped fresh parsley

900 ml (1½ pints) water

2 × 432 g (15 oz) cans of cannellini beans, drained

75 g (3 oz) breadcrumbs (optional)

salt and pepper

This delicious and filling dish is a simplification of the traditional French cassoulet. The main stew can be made 24 hours in advance, but it should be reheated before the final layer of breadcrumbs is added. Though the breadcrumbs bake to a lovely crisp layer which contrasts well with the stew, they're not absolutely necessary, and the cassoulet will still taste good without them. You need a large flameproof casserole for this recipe, or you can assemble the dish in a saucepan, then transfer it to an ovenproof dish to cook. Serve with a large green salad.

Heat the oil in a very large pan or flameproof casserole and add the chicken. Fry over a high heat until browned, then remove from the pan and reserve. Add the bacon, onion and carrot to the oil remaining in the pan and fry until they are beginning to brown.

Turn down the heat and add the garlic. Cook for 1–2 minutes, then return the chicken to the pan together with the passata, tomato purée, sugar, bay leaf, thyme, rosemary and half the parsley. Cook over a moderate heat for 3–4 minutes, stirring occasionally. Add the water and cannellini beans, season with salt and pepper, and bring to the boil. Reduce the heat and simmer very gently, half covered, for 40 minutes. Crush some of the beans against the side of the pan to thicken the sauce, stirring them in as you crush them. Taste and adjust the seasoning, and transfer to an ovenproof dish if cooked in a pan.

Preheat the oven to Gas Mark 5/190°C/375°F. Mix the breadcrumbs with the remaining parsley and spread in a thick layer over the surface of the cassoulet. Bake in the oven for 30–40 minutes or until the crust is browned. Serve piping hot.

VEGETABLE COUSCOUS

Preparation and cooking time: 1¾–2 hours   Serves 8

250 g (8 oz) onions, chopped

375 g (12 oz) carrots, sliced thickly

375 g (12 oz) pumpkin or butternut squash, peeled, de-seeded and cubed

250 g (8 oz) turnips, peeled and cubed

250 g (8 oz) cooked chick-peas, or 200 g (7 oz) canned chick-peas, drained

500 g (1 lb) courgettes, sliced thickly

1 aubergine, cubed

1–2 fennel bulbs, chopped roughly

2 fresh green chillies, de-seeded and chopped

250–375 g (8–12 oz) tomatoes, skinned and chopped, or a 397 g (14 oz) can of chopped tomatoes

125 g (4 oz) dried apricots, cut into strips

1 tablespoon paprika

½ teaspoon ground ginger

a handful of fresh parsley, chopped finely

salt

For the couscous:

500 g (1 lb) couscous

50 g (2 oz) butter, diced

chopped fresh coriander, to serve (optional)

Couscous is a type of grain, or more technically a type of pasta, since the grains of semolina are rolled in flour, though you wouldn't know to look at it. The word has also come to mean the combination of the cooked grain with the mildly spiced stew that is served with it. This is an all-vegetable version of couscous. You don't have to stick with the vegetables I've suggested here – choose according to what's available. If you haven't got one very large (4.5-litre/8-pint) saucepan, use two smaller ones.

If you can't find any couscous, then you can serve the stew with plain boiled rice instead.

Put the onions, carrots, pumpkin or squash and turnips in a very large saucepan and pour over water to cover. Bring to the boil, then reduce the heat and simmer for 15 minutes. Add the remaining stew ingredients, season with salt, and add more water to cover. Bring back to the boil and simmer for 45 minutes. Taste and adjust the seasoning.

While the stew is cooking, preheat the oven to Gas Mark 5/190°C/375°F. Measure the volume of couscous in a measuring jug and put it in a bowl. Pour over an equal volume of warm water (about 650 ml/22 fl oz). Stir and set aside for 15 minutes or until the water has been absorbed. Season with salt and pile into a large serving dish. Dot butter all over the surface of the couscous, then cover loosely with foil. Heat through in the oven for about 30 minutes or until piping hot. Sprinkle with chopped coriander, if available, and serve with the stew.

Vegetable Couscous

TAHINASALAT

Preparation time: 10 minutes   Serves 6–8

about 150 g (5 oz) tahina
paste

2 garlic cloves, crushed

juice of 1–1½ lemons

4–5 tablespoons cold water

2 tablespoons chopped fresh
parsley

salt

To serve:

olive or sunflower oil

ground cumin and chilli
powder (optional)

Though the name suggests a salad, this is actually one of the quickest of dips to throw together. It's based on tahina, a sesame seed paste which can be bought in jars. Before you measure out the quantity of tahina needed, stir it well to re-mix the oil which will have separated out. Don't worry when the tahina seizes up like cement; as you continue adding liquid and beating, it will smooth out again. This dip can be made up to two days in advance and stored, covered, in the fridge. Serve with warm pitta bread, bread sticks and crudités, i.e. raw salad vegetables, such as radishes, carrots, peppers, courgettes, spring onions, etc., the larger ones cut into sticks.

Put the tahina in a bowl and add the garlic and the juice of ½ a lemon. Beat to mix, then stir in the juice of another ½ lemon. Start beating in the cold water, a tablespoon at a time, until the mixture becomes a smooth, pale cream. It should be thick enough to cling to, say, a stick of celery when dipped in, but moderately runny so that you don't remove huge dollops with each dip. Taste and add extra lemon juice and salt as needed. Stir in the parsley. To serve, drizzle a small amount of oil over the top and dust lightly with cumin and chilli power, if using.

INDEX TO RECIPES

Cover design: Barry Lowenhoff
Cover illustration: Sally Swabey
Text design: Ken Vail Graphic Design
Photography: Jess Koppel
Stylist: Antonia Gaunt
Food preparation: Mandy Wagstaff
Illustration: John Woodcock
Typesetting: Ace Filmsetting Ltd